Installing and Configuring Windows 10
Exam 70-698

Lab Manual

Patrick Regan

WILEY

SENIOR EXECUTIVE EDITOR   Bryan Gambrel
MARKET SOLUTIONS ASSISTANT   Jessy Moor
EXECUTIVE MARKETING MANAGER   Michele Szczesniak
CONTENT MANAGER   Nichole Urban
PRODUCTION COORDINATOR   Nicole Repasky
PRODUCTION EDITOR   Umamaheswari Gnanamani

www.wiley.com/college/microsoft

ISBN   978-1-119-35323-2

BRIEF CONTENTS

Lab 1: Preparing for Installation Requirements

Lab 2: Installing Windows

Lab 3: Configuring Devices and Device Drivers

Lab 4: Performing Post-Installation Configuration

Lab 5: Implementing Windows in an Enterprise Environment

Lab 6: Configuring Networking

Lab 7: Configuring Storage

Lab 8: Configuring Data Access and Usage

Lab 9: Implementing Apps

Lab 10: Configuring Remote Management

Lab 11: Configuring Updates

Lab 12: Monitoring Windows

Lab 13: Configuring System and Data Recovery

Lab 14: Configuring Authorization and Authentication

Lab 15: Configuring Advanced Management Tools

CONTENTS

1. **Preparing for Installation Requirements**   **1**

    Exercise 1.1:   Creating Windows 10 Installation Media 2

    Lab Challenge: Preparing for Windows 10 Installation 4

2. **Installing Windows**   **7**

    Exercise 2.1:   Installing Windows 10 8

    Exercise 2.2:   Upgrading Windows 10 10

    Exercise 2.3:   Installing the User State Migration Tool 13

    Exercise 2.4:   Migrating User Profiles 14

    Lab Challenge: Installing 10 Additional Windows 10 Features 18

3. **Configuring Devices and Device Drivers**   **21**

    Exercise 3.1:   Creating a VHD Boot File Using Disk Management 22

    Exercise 3.2:   Working with Device Manager 24

    Lab Challenge: Rolling Back a Device Driver 28

4. **Performing Post-Installation Configuration**   **31**

    Exercise 4.1:   Configuring Windows 10 32

    Exercise 4.2:   Configuring Power Settings 35

    Exercise 4.3:   Configuring Internet Explorer 37

    Exercise 4.4:   Installing Hyper-V 40

    Exercise 4.5:   Creating and Managing Virtual Machines 41

    Lab Challenge: Configuring Microsoft Edge 46

5. **Implementing Windows in an Enterprise Environment**   **49**

    Exercise 5.1:   Installing the Windows Assessment and Deployment Kit 51

    Exercise 5.2:   Creating a Provisioning Package with the Windows Imaging and Configuration Designer Tool 52

    Exercise 5.3:   Configuring Group Policy 55

    Lab Challenge: Configuring User Account Control (UAC) 56

6. **Configuring Networking**   **59**

    Exercise 6.1:   Configuring IPv4 Settings 60

    Exercise 6.2:   Configuring IPv6 Settings 63

    Exercise 6.3:   Configuring Advanced Shared Settings for Network Locations 64

    Exercise 6.4:   Configuring Windows Firewall 66

    Exercise 6.5:   Configuring a VPN Client 68

    Lab Challenge: Configuring Wi-Fi Networking 71

7. **Configuring Storage**   **75**

    Exercise 7.1:   Creating a Simple Volume 76

    Exercise 7.2:   Creating a Storage Pool and a Storage Space 78

    Lab Challenge: Using Windows PowerShell to Configure Disks 80

v

8. Configuring Data Access and Usage   **81**

Exercise 8.1:   Managing NTFS and Share Permissions 82
Exercise 8.2:   Configuring Libraries 85
Exercise 8.3:   Configuring Printers 87
Exercise 8.4:   Supporting HomeGroups 90
Lab Challenge: Using OneDrive to Manage Files/Folders 91

9. Implementing Apps   **95**

Exercise 9.1:   Signing Up for Microsoft Intune 96
Exercise 9.2:   Sideloading a Windows Store App to Microsoft Intune 100
Exercise 9.3:   Managing Default Apps 102
Exercise 9.4:   Managing Desktop Applications 103
Lab Challenge: Managing Windows Store Apps 105

10. Configuring Remote Management   **109**

Exercise 10.1:   Configuring Remote Desktop 110
Exercise 10.2:   Configuring Remote Assistance 113
Exercise 10.3:   Managing a Remote System using the Microsoft Management Console 115
Lab Challenge: Running PowerShell Commands on a Remote Computer 117

11. Configuring Updates   **121**

Exercise 11.1:   Configuring Windows 10 Updates 122
Lab Challenge: Configuring Windows Update Policies 124

12. Monitoring Windows   **127**

Exercise 12.1:   Using Event Viewer 128
Exercise 12.2:   Using Reliability Monitor 134
Exercise 12.3:   Using Task Manager 135

Exercise 12.4:   Using Resource Monitor 138
Exercise 12.5:   Using Performance Monitor 139
Lab Challenge: Configuring Indexing Options 142

13. Configuring System and Data Recovery   **145**

Exercise 13.1:   Configuring Windows Defender 146
Exercise 13.2:   Configuring a Restore Point 148
Exercise 13.3:   Scheduling a Windows 10 Backup 150
Exercise 13.4:   Performing a File Restore 152
Exercise 13.5:   Using File History 154
Lab Challenge: Recovering Files from OneDrive 156

14. Configuring Authorization and Authentication   **159**

Exercise 14.1:   Creating a Local User Account 160
Exercise 14.2:   Configuring a PIN and Picture Password 163
Exercise 14.3:   Creating and Managing Domain User Accounts 167
Exercise 14.4:   Using Credential Manager 169
Exercise 14.5:   Configuring Device Guard and Credential Guard 171
Lab Challenge: Managing Account Policies 173

15. Configuring Advanced Management Tools   **177**

Exercise 15.1:   Configuring Services 178
Exercise 15.2:   Using System Configuration Management Utility 181
Exercise 15.3:   Using Task Scheduler 182
Lab Challenge: Creating a Windows PowerShell Script 184

LAB 1
PREPARING FOR INSTALLATION REQUIREMENTS

THIS LAB CONTAINS THE FOLLOWING EXERCISES AND ACTIVITIES:

Exercise 1.1   Creating Windows 10 Installation Media

Lab Challenge   Preparing for Windows 10 Installation

BEFORE YOU BEGIN

The lab environment consists of student workstations connected to a local area network, along with a server that functions as the domain controller for a domain called adatum.com. The computers required for this lab are listed in Table 1-1.

Table 1-1
Computers required for Lab 1

Computer	Operating System	Computer Name
Client (VM 1)	Windows 10	Computer with connection to the Internet.

In addition to the computers, you will also require the software listed in Table 1-2 to complete Lab 1.

Table 1-2
Software required for Lab 1

Software	Location
Lab 1 student worksheet	Lab01_worksheet.docx (provided by instructor)

Working with Lab Worksheets

Each lab in this manual requires that you answer questions, shoot screen shots, and perform other activities that you will document in a worksheet named for the lab, such as Lab01_worksheet.docx. You will find these worksheets on the book companion site. It is recommended that you use a USB flash drive to store your worksheets, so you can submit them to your instructor for review. As you perform the exercises in each lab, open the appropriate worksheet file, fill in the required information, and then save the file to your flash drive.

SCENARIO

After completing this lab, you will be able to:

- Create installation media

- Determine hardware requirements and compatibility

- Choose between an upgrade and a clean installation

Estimated lab time: 50 minutes

Exercise 1.1	Creating Windows 10 Installation Media
Overview	In this exercise, you will create Windows 10 Installation Media on a USB drive.
Mindset	Traditional Windows was installed with an installation DVD that was purchased or downloaded as an ISO file and burned to a DVD. With Windows 10, you can place the Windows installation on a USB device. To perform the installation, simply connect and boot from the USB device. As such, you can perform a Windows installation from a USB device or bootable DVD disk.
Completion time	40 minutes

NOTE	*You will not be able to perform these labs on the MOAC Labs Online systems. Instead, you need to use a computer running Windows 10 with access to the Internet. If your classroom has a dedicated Windows Server 2012 R2 or Windows Server 2016, you can use a virtual machine running Windows 10.*

1. Log in to a computer running Windows 10 that is connected to the Interent.

2. Click the **Start** button and type **IExplore**. Then from the search results, click **Internet Explorer**.

3. In Internet Explorer, open your favorite search engine and search for **Windows 10 Media Creation Tool**. Click for the first page hosted by www.microsoft.com.

4. Scroll down and click **Download tool now**.

5. When you are prompted to confirm that you want to run or save MediaCreationTool.exe file, click **Run**. If you are prompted to allow this app to make changes to your PC, click **Yes**.

6. In Windows 10 Setup, on the License terms page, click **Accept**.

7. On the What do you want to do? Page, select **Create installation media for another PC** and then click **Next**.

8. On the Select English, architecture, and edition page (as shown in Figure 1-1), select **English** (**United States**). Then for the architecture, select **Both**. Click **Next**.

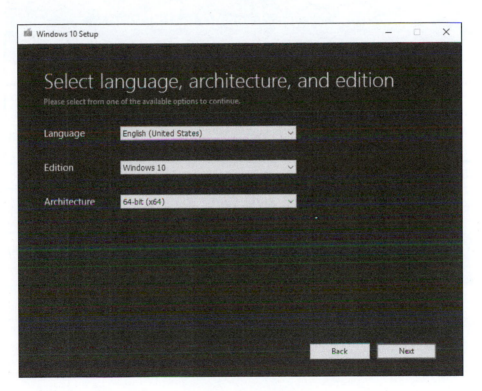

Figure 1-1
Selecting images to use

9. On the Choose which media to use page, select **ISO file** and then click **Next**.

10. In the Select a path dialog box, answer the following question, and then for the File name, type **Windows10Install.iso** and click **Save**.

Question 1	What is the default folder that the ISO file will be saved to?

11. When the necessary files have been downloaded and the ISO file has been created, take a screen shot of the Windows 10 Setup page by pressing **Alt+PrtScr** and then paste it into your Lab01_ worksheet file in the page provided by pressing **Ctrl+V**.

12. Click **Finish**.

Question 2	What is the next step necessary in order for the ISO file to install Windows?

Log off the computer running Windows 10.

Lab Challenge	Preparing for Windows 10 Installation
Overview	In this exercise, you will be asked a series of questions that will review the installation requirements for Windows 10.
Mindset	To determine what you need to install Windows 10, you also need to look at the minimum system requirements for Windows 10. You should also determine whether your system is compatible with your current hardware or the hardware you are about to purchase.
Completion time	10 minutes

Question 3	What is the minimum memory and processor needed to run a 32-bit version of Windows 10.

Question 4	How much memory is needed to run a 64-bit version of Windows 10?

Question 5	To which version of Windows 10 can you upgrade a workstation running Windows 7 Professional, 64-bit?

Question 6	You administer a computer running Windows 8.1 Enterprise running several applications. To upgrade to Windows 10 Pro, which type of installation is necessary?

Question 7	Which versions of Windows 10 supports Windows Hello?

Question 8	You are running Windows 10 Professional. Which editions of Windows 10 can you connect to using Remote Desktop?

You administer a network of about 450 users using a mix of desktop and laptops running Windows 10. Answer the following questions.

End of lab.

LAB 2
INSTALLING WINDOWS

THIS LAB CONTAINS THE FOLLOWING EXERCISES AND ACTIVITIES:

Exercise 2.1   Installing Windows 10

Exercise 2.2   Upgrading Windows 10

Exercise 2.3   Installing the User State Migration Tool

Exercise 2.4   Migrating User Profiles

Lab Challenge   Installing Additional Windows 10 Features

BEFORE YOU BEGIN

The lab environment consists of student workstations connected to a local area network, along with a server that functions as the domain controller for a domain called adatum.com. The computers required for this lab are listed in Table 2-1.

Table 2-1
Computers required for Lab 2

Computer	Operating System	Computer Name
Server (VM 1)	Windows Server 2012 R2	LON-DC1
Client (VM 3)	Windows 10	LON-CL1
Client (VM 4)	Windows 10	LON-CL2
Client (VM 5)	Windows 10	LON-CL3
Client (VM 6)	Windows 10	LON-CL5

In addition to the computers, you will also require the software listed in Table 2-2 to complete Lab 2.

Table 2-2
Software required for Lab 2

Software	Location
Lab 2 student worksheet	Lab02_worksheet.docx (provided by instructor)

Working with Lab Worksheets

Each lab in this manual requires that you answer questions, shoot screen shots, and perform other activities that you will document in a worksheet named for the lab, such as Lab02_worksheet.docx. You will find these worksheets on the book companion site. It is recommended that you use a USB flash drive to store your worksheets, so you can submit them to your instructor for review. As you perform the exercises in each lab, open the appropriate worksheet file, fill in the required information, and then save the file to your flash drive.

SCENARIO

After completing this lab, you will be able to:

- ▪ Install Windows

- ▪ Upgrade Windows 10

- ▪ Install the User State Migration Tool

- ▪ Migrate User Profiles

- ▪ Install additional Windows 10 features

Estimated lab time: 120 minutes

Exercise 2.1	Installing Windows 10
Overview	In this exercise, you will complete the installation of Windows 10. Normally, you would insert the installation disk into the DVD drive and boot the system from the disk.
Mindset	The simplest way to perform a clean install (a new installation) of Windows 10 is to boot from bootable Windows 10 installation disk or USB drive, which will start the setup program.
Completion time	20 minutes

1. On LON-CL5, you should already be at the Windows Setup screen, as shown in Figure 2-1. With the Language to install, Time and currency format, and Keyboard or input method already selected for you on the screen, click **Next**.

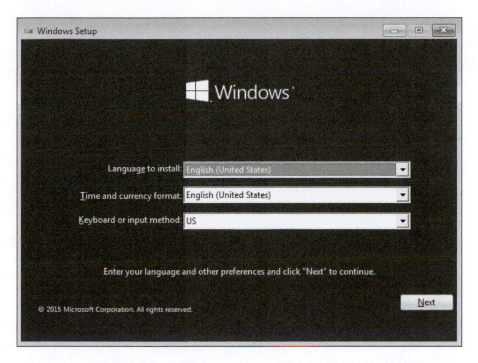

Figure 2-1
The initial Windows Setup screen

2. Click **Install now**.

3. On the License Terms page, select the I accept the license terms option and then click **Next**.

4. Click the **Custom: Install Windows only (advanced)** option.

5. When you are prompted to indicate where to install Windows, Drive 0 Partition 2 is already selected. Click **Next**.

6. If a message displays, indicating that there are previous Windows installations, click **OK**.

7. The installation will take several minutes. After the virtual machine reboots, on the Get going fast page, click **Use Express settings**.

8. On the Create an account for this PC page, in the Who's going to use this PC text box, type **Admin**.

9. In the Enter password text box and the Re-enter password text box, type **Pa$$w0rd**. In the Password hint text box, type **Default**. Click **Next**.

10. Right-click the **Start** button and choose **System**. The System page opens.

Question 1	*Which edition of Windows are you running?*

Question 2	*Is this a 32-bit edition of Windows or is it a 64-bit edition of Windows?*

11. Click the **Change settings** option.

12. Click the **Change** button.

13. In the System Properties dialog box, click the **Change** button.

14. In the Computer name text box, type **LON-CL5**.

15. Select the Domain option. Then in the Domain text box, type **adatum** and click **OK**.

16. In the Windows Security dialog box, in the User name text box, type **Administrator**. In the Password text box, type **Pa$$w0rd**, and click **OK**.

17. When a dialog box appears, welcoming you to the adatum domain, take a screen shot showing a successful configuration of a Windows desktop by pressing **Alt+PrtScr** and then paste it into your Lab02_worksheet file in the page provided by pressing **Ctrl+V**.

18. Click **OK** to close the dialog box.

19. Click **OK** to restart Windows.

20. Click **Close** to close the System Properties dialog box.

21. In the Microsoft Windows dialog box, click **Restart Now**.

You will not be using LON-CL5 in the future exercises.

Exercise 2.2	Upgrading Windows 10
Overview	In this exercise, you will upgrade a virtual machine running Windows 7 to Windows 10. The installation DVD is already placed in the virtual DVD drive (drive D).
Mindset	When you need to upgrade from Windows 7 or Windows 8/8.1, you can navigate to https://www.microsoft.com/en-us/software-download/windows10 and click the Download Tool now button. You can then launch the Download Tool to create an installation media or to upgrade a PC with the older operating system.
Completion time	20 minutes

1. Log on to **LON-CL3** as **adatum\administrator** with the password of **Pa$$w0rd**.

2. Click the **Start** button and then click **Computer**. The Computer window opens, as shown in Figure 2-2.

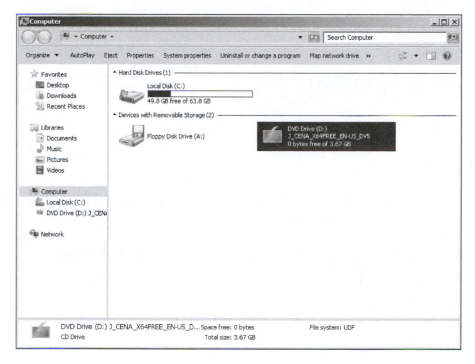

Figure 2-2
Opening the Computer window.

3. Double-click the **D drive** and then double-click **setup.exe**. (When you are prompted to get important updates, it is usually best to use the Downlad and install update options.) For our lab, you will click the **Not right now** option and then click **Next**.

4. On the License terms page, click **Accept**.

5. On the Choose what to keep page, answer the following question and then click **Next**.

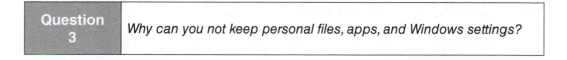

Question 3	*Why can you not keep personal files, apps, and Windows settings?*

6. When you are prompted to continue using this selection, click **Yes**. The Ready to install page opens.

Question 4	Which edition of Windows are you installing?

7. Click **Install**.

8. On the Hi there page, click **Next**.

9. On the Get going fast page, click **Use Express settings**.

10. On the Create an account for this PC page, in the Who's going to use this PC text box, type **Admin**.

11. On the Enter password text box and the Re-enter password text box, type **Pa$$w0rd**. In the Password hint text box, type **Default**. Click **Next**.

12. When the desktop appears, right-click the **Start** button and choose **System**.

Question 5	Which edition of Windows are you running?

Question 6	Is this a 32-bit edition of Windows or is it a 64-bit edition of Windows?

13. Click the **Change settings** option.

14. In the System Properties dialog box, click the **Change** button.

15. In the Computer name text box, type **LON-CL3**.

16. Select the Domain option. Then in the Domain text box, type **adatum** and click **OK**.

17. In the Windows Security dialog box, in the User name text box, type **Administrator**. In the Password text box, type **Pa$$w0rd** and then click **OK**.

18. When a dialog box appears, welcoming you to the adatum domain, take a screen shot showing a successful configuration of a Windows desktop by pressing **Alt+PrtScr** and then paste it into your Lab02_worksheet file in the page provided by pressing **Ctrl+V**.

Log off LON-CL3.

Exercise 2.3	Installing the User State Migration Tool
Overview	In this exercise, you will install the User State Migration Tool (USMT), which is part of the Windows Assessment and Deployment Kit.
Mindset	One of the most time-consuming tasks you will perform as an administrator is moving user files and settings between computers and operating systems. The USMT eases this burden.
Completion time	10 minutes

1. Log on to **LON-DC1** as **adatum\administrator** with the password of **Pa$$w0rd**.

2. On **LON-DC1** open File Explorer by clicking the **File Explorer** icon on the taskbar.

3. In File Explorer, navigate to **C:\Software** and find adksetup.exe (as shown in Figure 2-3). Double-click **adksetup.exe**.

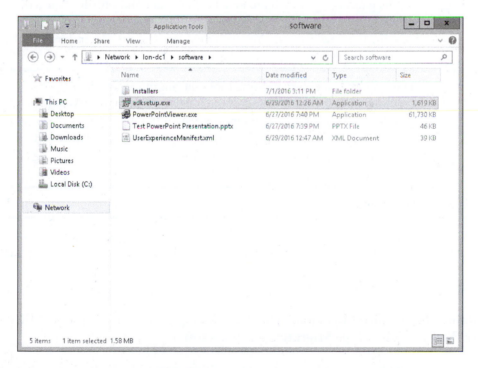

Figure 2-3
Accessing the ADK software folder

4. In the Windows Assessment and Deployment Kit – Windows 10 window, on the Specify Location page, click **Next**.

5. On the Windows Kits Privacy page, click **Next**.

6. On the License Agreement page, click **Accept**.

7. On the Select the features you want to install option, deselect all options except the User State Migration Tool (USMT) and then click **Install**.

8. When USMT is installed, take a screen shot of Welcome screen by pressing **Alt+PrtScr** and then paste it into your Lab02_worksheet file in the page provided by pressing **Ctrl+V**.

9. Click **Close**.

Remain logged in to LON-DC1 for the next exercise.

Exercise 2.4	Migrating User Profiles
Overview	In this exercise, you will create a new account and profile. You will then use the User State Migration Tool (USMT) to back up the user data for the new account. You will then delete a profile and restore the profile from the backup.
Mindset	The USMT is a command-line tool that migrates user data from a previous installation of Windows to a new installation of Windows. The ScanState.exe program scans the source computer, collects the files and settings, and then creates a store that contains the user's files and settings. The LoadState.exe program restores the files and settings on the destination computer.
Completion time	60 minutes

1. On LON-DC1, open File Explorer by clicking the **File Explorer** icon on the taskbar.

2. Double-click **Local Disk (C:)**.

3. To create a folder called Migration, right-click the empty white space of **Local Disk (C:)** and choose **New > Folder**. Type **Migration** and press **Enter**.

4. Using the same method as the last step, create a folder named **C:\Data**.

5. Right-click the **Migration** folder and choose **Properties**.

6. Click the **Sharing** tab, as shown in Figure 2-4.

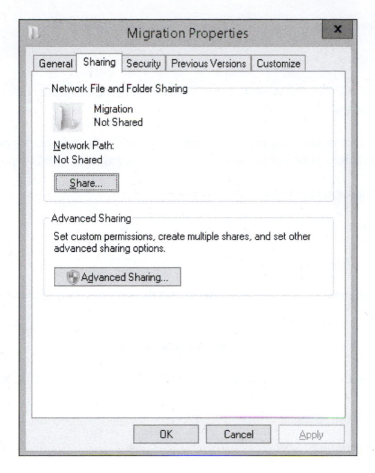

Figure 2-4
Configuring sharing of the Migration folder

7. Click the **Advanced Sharing** button.

8. In the Advanced Sharing dialog box, click the **Share this folder**.

9. Click **Permissions**.

10. In the Permissions for Migration dialog box, with Everyone selected, click to select **Allow Full Control** and then click **OK**.

11. Close the Advanced Sharing dialog box by clicking **OK**.

12. Close the Migration Properties dialog box by clicking **Close**.

13. Right-click the **Data** folder and choose **Properties**.

14. Click the **Sharing** tab.

15. In the Data Properties dialog box, click the **Advanced Sharing** button.

16. In the Advanced Sharing dialog box, click the **Share this folder**.

17. Click **Permissions**.

18. In the Permissions for Migration dialog box, with Everyone selected, click to select **Allow Full Control**

19. Take a screen shot of showing the share permissions of the Data folder by pressing **Alt+PrtScr** and then paste it into your Lab02_worksheet file in the page provided by pressing **Ctrl+V**.

20. Close the Permissions for Data folder by clicking **OK**.

21. Close the Advanced Sharing dialog box by clicking **OK**.

22. Close the Data Properties dialog box by clicking **Close**.

23. Using Server Manager, click the **Tools** menu and then choose **Active Directory Users and Computers**.

24. Right-click the **Users** organizational unit and choose **New > User**.

25. In the New Object – user dialog box, specify the following and then click **Next**:

    First name: **Jim**

    Last name: **Austin**

    Full name: **Jim Austin**

    User logon name: **JAustin**

26. In the Password text box and the Confirm password text box, type **Pa$$w0rd**.

27. Click to select **Password never expires**. In the Active Directory Domain Services dialog box, click **OK** and then click **Next**.

28. When the wizard finishes, click **Finish**.

29. Log on to **LON-CL2** as **adatum\JAustin** with the password of **Pa$$w0rd**.

30. Right-click the **Desktop** and choose **New > Text Document**. Name the document **Lab2**.

31. Log off **LON-CL2**.

32. Log on to **LON-CL2** as **adatum\administrator** with the password of **Pa$$w0rd**.

33. Open **File Explorer** and click **This PC**.

34. Click the Computer tab, as shown in Figure 2-5, and then click **Map network drive**.

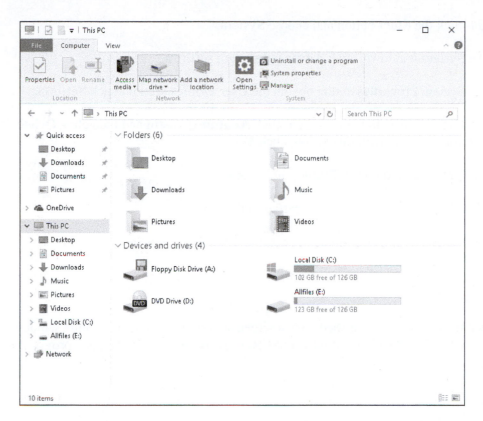

Figure 2-5
Mapping drives in Windows 10

35. In the Map Network Drive window, for Drive, select **M:**. Then in the Folder text box, type **\\ LON-DC1\C$\Program Files (x86)\Windows Kits\10\Assessment and Deployment Kit**. Click **Finish**.

36. Right-click the Start button, and select **Command Prompt (Admin)**.

37. In the Administrator: Command Prompt window, type **m:** and then press **Enter**. Then from the M drive, type **CD User State Migration Tool\amd64** and press **Enter**.

38. At the command prompt, execute the following command:

```
scanstate \ue:*\* /ui:adatum\JAustin \\LON-DC1\data /i:migapp.xml
/i:miguser.xml /o /vsc /efs:copyraw /c
```

Question 7	What does the efs:copyraw option do?

39. When the migration is finished, take a screen shot of the command prompt window by pressing **Alt+PrtScr** and then paste it into your Lab02_worksheet file in the page provided by pressing **Ctrl+V**.

40. Right-click the **Start** button and choose **System**.

41. In the System windows, click **Advanced system settings**.

42. In the System Properties dialog box, in the User Profiles section, click **Settings**.

43. In the User Profiles dialog box open, click **Adatum\JAustin** and then click **Delete**. When you are prompted to confirm this action, click **Yes**.

44. Click **OK** to close the User Profiles dialog box.

45. Click **OK** to close the System Properties dialog box.

46. Return to the command prompt and execute following command:

```
Loadstate /ui:adatum\jaustin \\LON-DC1\data /i:migapp.xml
/i:miguser.xml
```

47. When the migration is finished, take a screen shot of the command prompt window by pressing **Alt+PrtScr** and then paste it into your Lab02_worksheet file in the page provided by pressing **Ctrl+V**.

48. Log off **LON-CL2**.

49. Log on to **LON-CL2** as **adatum\JAustin** with the password of **Pa$$w0rd**.

50. Verify that the Lab02 document is located on the Desktop.

51. Log off **LON-CL2**.

52. Log off **LON-DC1**.

Lab Challenge	Installing 10 Additional Windows 10 Features
Overview	In this exercise, you will install the Telnet Client and Windows TIFF IFilter.
Mindset	Windows 10 has many optional features or built-in programs available that provide additional functionality. However, not all of the programs are available after the initial installation. Many of these features are built for business networks, which might not be useful for everyone. To install these additional features, open the Windows Features dialog box and turn on the appropriate feature.
Completion time	10 minutes

1. On LON-CL1, right-click the **Start** button and choose **Programs and Features**.

2. In the Programs and Features window, click **Turn Windows features on or off**.

Question 8	*Which version of .NET Framework is already installed?*

3. In the Windows Features window (as shown in Figure 2-6), scroll down and then select **Telnet Client** and **Windows TIFF IFilter**.

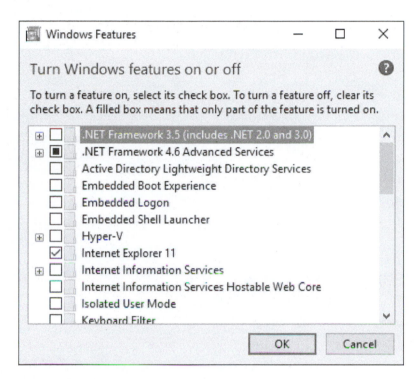

Figure 2-6
Mapping drives in Windows 10

4. To install the applications, click **OK**.

5. When the installation is complete, click **Close**.

6. Click the **Turn Windows featuers on or off** option.

7. Scroll down to the bottom of the Windows feature list.

8. Take a screen shot of the Windows Features window showing that Telnet Client and Windows TIFF IFilter are installed by pressing **Alt+PrtScr** and then paste it into your Lab02_worksheet file in the page provided by pressing **Ctrl+V**.

9. Click **Close**.

10. Close the Programs and Features page.

End of lab.

LAB 3
CONFIGURING DEVICES AND DEVICE DRIVERS

THIS LAB CONTAINS THE FOLLOWING EXERCISES AND ACTIVITIES:

Exercise 3.1   Creating a VHD Boot File Using Disk Management

Exercise 3.2   Working with Device Manager

Lab Challenge   Rolling Back a Device Driver

BEFORE YOU BEGIN

The lab environment consists of student workstations connected to a local area network, along with a server that functions as the domain controller for a domain called adatum.com. The computers required for this lab are listed in Table 3-1.

Table 3-1
Computers required for Lab 3

Computer	*Operating System*	*Computer Name*
Server (VM 1)	Windows Server 2012 R2	LON-DC1
Client (VM 2)	Windows 10	LON-CL1

In addition to the computers, you will also require the software listed in Table 3-2 to complete Lab 3.

Table 3-2
Software required for Lab 3

Software	Location
Lab 3 student worksheet	Lab03_worksheet.docx (provided by instructor)

Working with Lab Worksheets

Each lab in this manual requires that you answer questions, shoot screen shots, and perform other activities that you will document in a worksheet named for the lab, such as Lab03_worksheet.docx. You will find these worksheets on the book companion site. It is recommended that you use a USB flash drive to store your worksheets, so you can submit them to your instructor for review. As you perform the exercises in each lab, open the appropriate worksheet file, fill in the required information, and then save the file to your flash drive.

SCENARIO

After completing this lab, you will be able to:

■ Create a VHD boot file using Disk Management

■ Install, update, and disable drivers

■ Roll back a driver

Estimated lab time: 55 minutes

Exercise 3.1	Creating a VHD Boot File Using Disk Management
Overview	In this exercise, you will create a VHD boot file using Disk Management.
Mindset	A native VHD boot file allows you to mount and boot from the operating system contained within the VHD, which allows you to test the performance and compatibility on your current system. It can also be used to streamline image management.
Completion time	15 minutes

1. Log on to **LON-CL1** using the **adatum\administrator** account and the **Pa$$w0rd** password.

2. Right-click the **Start** button. Then, from the context menu that appears, choose **Disk Management**. The Computer Management console opens, as shown in Figure 3-1.

3. If an Initialize Disk dialog box displays, click the **Cancel** button.

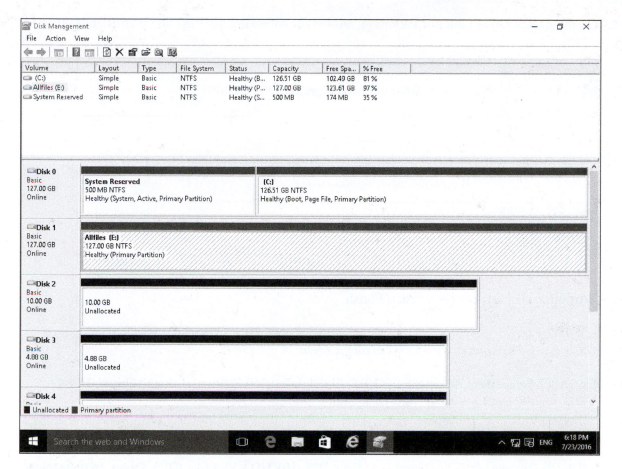

Figure 3-1
The Disk Management node

4. Click **Action > Create VHD**.

5. In the Location text box, type **C:\Win10VHDA**. For the Virtual hard disk size setting, specify **20 GB**. For the Virtual hard disk type setting, select **Dynamically expanding**.

6. Take a screen shot of the Create and Attach Virtual Hard Disk dialog box by pressing **Alt+PrtScr** and then paste it into your Lab03_worksheet file in the page provided by pressing **Ctrl+V**.

7. Click **OK** to close the Create and Attach Virtual Hard Disk dialog box.

8. Right-click the new disk (20.00 GB Unallocated disk) and choose **Initialize Disk**.

9. In the Initialize Disk dialog box, click **OK**.

10. Right-click the **Disk 5 Unallocated** disk space and choose **New Simple Volume**.

11. In the Welcome to the New Simple Volume Wizard, click **Next**.

12. On the Specify Volume Size page, click **Next**.

13. On the Assign Drive Letter or Path page, answer the following question and then click **Next**.

Question 1	Which drive letter will be assigned to the drive?

14. On the Format Partition page, answer the following question and then click **Next**.

Question 2	What is the default file system?

15. When the wizard is complete, click **Finish**.

16. If a dialog box displays, prompting you to format a disk, click **Cancel** to close the dialog box. Close any File Explorer windows that might open.

17. On Disk Management, to detach the VHD file, right-click the virtual disk and choose **Detach VHD**. On the Detach Virtual Hard Disk, dialog box, click **OK**.

18. To reattach the VHD file, click **Action > Attach VHD**.

19. Click the **Browse** button and browse to the **c:\Win10VHDA.vhd** file. Click **Open**. In the Attach Virtual Hard Disk dialog box, click **OK**.

Close Disk Management and any File Explorer windows, but leave the computer logged in for the next exercise.

Exercise 3.2	Working with Device Manager
Overview	In this exercise, you will update device drivers with Device Manager.
Mindset	Device Manager provides you with a graphical tool to manage devices and device drivers.
Completion time	35 minutes

1. On LON-CL1, right-click the **Start button** and choose **Device Manager**.

Question 3	Are there any errors or unknown devices?

2. Expand the **Ports (COM & LPT)** node (see Figure 3-2).

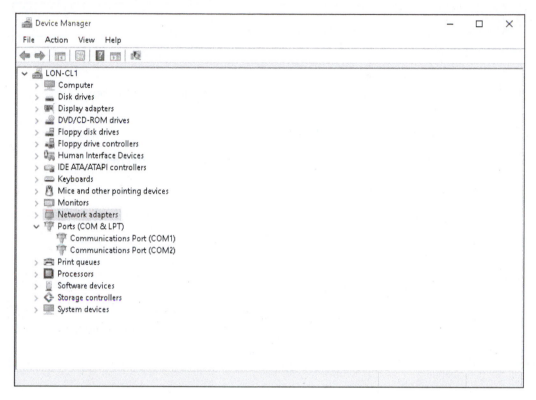

Figure 3-2
Expanding the Ports (COM & LPT) node

3. Right-click **Communications Port (COM2)** and choose **Disable**.

4. When you are prompted to confirm that you want to disable the device, click **Yes**.

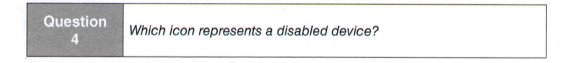

Question 4	Which icon represents a disabled device?

5. Right-click **Communications Port (COM2)** and choose **Enable**.

6. Right-click **Communications Port (COM2)** and choose **Properties**.

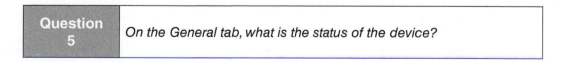

Question 5	On the General tab, what is the status of the device?

7. Click the **Resources** tab.

Question 6	What IRQ and I/O port range is Com2 using?

8. Click **OK** to close the Communications Port (COM2) Properties dialog box.

9. Expand the **Floppy drive controllers** node.

10. Right-click the **Standard floppy disk controller** and choose **Properties**.

Question 7	On the General tab, what is the status of the device?

11. Click the **Resources** tab.

Question 8	Which IRQ, DMA, and I/O port ranges are used by the Standard floppy disk controller?

12. Click to deselect the **Use automatic settings**.

Note	This exercise is for demonstration purposes only. In today's computing environment, you almost never need to manually configure these settings.

13. Change the Setting based on setting to **Basic configuration 0002**.

14. Double-click **IRQ**. In the Edit Interrupt Request dialog box, change the Value to **05**. Click **OK** to close the Edit Interrupt Request dialog box.

15. Click **OK** to close the Standard floppy disk controller Properties dialog box.

16. When you are prompted to confirm that you want to continue, click **Yes**.

17. When you are prompted to restart the computer, click **No**.

Question 9	Which icon is shown by the Standard floppy disk controller now?

18. Double-click **Standard floppy disk controller**.

Question 10	What is the device status now?

19. Click the **Resources** tab.

20. Click **Set Configuration Manually**.

21. Click to select **Use automatic settings**.

22. Click **OK** to close the Standard floppy disk controller Properties dialog box.

23. When you are prompted to restart the computer, click **Yes**.

24. Log on to **LON-CL1** using the **adatum\administrator** account and the **Pa$$w0rd** password.

25. Right-click the **Start button** and choose **Device Manager**.

26. Right-click **LON-CL1** and choose **Scan for hardware changes**.

27. Expand the **Ports (COM and LPT)** node and then click **Communications Port (COM2) port**.

28. Right-click **Communications Port (COM2) port** and choose **Update Driver Software**.

29. On the How do you want to search for driver software? page, click **Search automatically for updated driver software**.

Question 11	Which driver was located and what information was provided about the driver?

30. Click **Close** to close the Update Driver Software – Communications Port (COM2) dialog box.

31. Right-click **Communications port (COM2)** and choose **Properties**.

32. Click the **Driver** tab.

Question 12	Which driver version is being used by Communication Port (COM2)?

33. Click **Update Driver**.

34. On the How do you want to search for driver software? page, click **Browse my computer for driver software**.

35. On the Browse for driver software on your computer page, click **Let me pick from a list of device drivers on my computer**.

36. On the Select the device driver you want to install for this hardware page, click to deselect the **Show compatible hardware**.

NOTE	*However, this is for demonstration purposes only. Normally, you want to use drivers that are compatible.*

37. For the Manufacturer, click **Trimble** and then click **Trimble PCMCIA GPS Adapter (Rev. B)**. Click **Next**.

38. 38. When an update driver warning is displayed, click **Yes**.

39. When the driver has been installed, click **Close**.

40. Take a screen shot of Device Manager by pressing **Alt+PrtScr** and then paste it into your Lab03_worksheet file in the page provided by pressing **Ctrl+V**.

End of exercise. Leave the Device Manager open for the next exercise.

Lab Challenge	Rolling Back a Device Driver
Overview	In this exercise, you will use Device Manager to roll back a device driver.
Mindset	Sometimes when you upgrade or load a device driver, the device for which the device driver is used stops working or causes other problems with Windows. With Device Manager, you can roll back a device driver to the previous device driver.
Completion time	5 minutes

1. On **LON-CL1**, using Device Manager, right-click **Trimble PCMCIA GPS Adapter (Rev. B) (COM2)** and choose **Properties**. The Trimble PCMCIA GPS Adapter (Rev. B) (COM2) Properties dialog box opens.

2. Click the **Driver** tab, as shown in Figure 3-3.

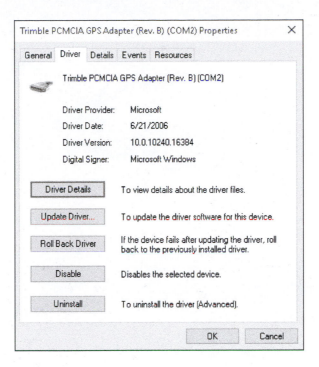

Figure 3-3
Managing drivers

3. Click **Roll Back Driver**.

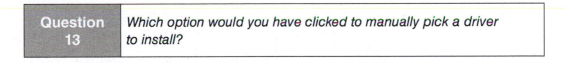

Question 13	Which option would you have clicked to manually pick a driver to install?

4. When you are prompted to confirm that you are sure you would like to roll back to the previously installed driver software, click **Yes**.

5. Take a screen shot of the Communications Port (COM2) Properties dialog box by pressing **Alt+PrtScr** and then paste it into your Lab03_worksheet file in the page provided by pressing **Ctrl+V**.

6. Click **Close** to close the Communications Port (COM2) Properties dialog box.

7. Close **Device Manager** and log off **LON-CL1**.

End of lab.

LAB 4
PERFORMING POST-INSTALLATION CONFIGURATION

THIS LAB CONTAINS THE FOLLOWING EXERCISES AND ACTIVITIES:

Exercise 4.1   Configuring Windows 10

Exercise 4.2   Configuring Power Settings

Exercise 4.3   Configuring Internet Explorer

Exercise 4.4   Installing Hyper-V

Exercise 4.5   Creating and Managing Virtual Machines

Lab Challenge   Configuring Microsoft Edge

BEFORE YOU BEGIN

The lab environment consists of student workstations connected to a local area network, along with a server that functions as the domain controller for a domain called adatum.com. The computers required for this lab are listed in Table 4-1.

Table 4-1
Computers required for Lab 4

Computer	Operating System	Computer Name
Server (VM 1)	Windows Server 2012 R2	LON-DC1
Client (VM 2)	Windows 10	LON-CL1

In addition to the computers, you will also require the software listed in Table 4-2 to complete Lab 4.

Table 4-2
Software required for Lab 4

Software	Location
Lab 4 student worksheet	Lab04_worksheet.docx (provided by instructor)

Working with Lab Worksheets

Each lab in this manual requires that you answer questions, shoot screen shots, and perform other activities that you will document in a worksheet named for the lab, such as Lab04_worksheet.docx. You will find these worksheets on the book companion site. It is recommended that you use a USB flash drive to store your worksheets, so you can submit them to your instructor for review. As you perform the exercises in each lab, open the appropriate worksheet file, fill in the required information, and then save the file to your flash drive.

SCENARIO

After completing this lab, you will be able to:

- Configure Windows 10

- Configure power settings

- Configure Internet Explorer

- Configure Microsoft Edge

- Install Hyper-V

- Create and manage virtual machines

Estimated lab time: 125 minutes

Exercise 4.1	Configuring Windows 10
Overview	In this exercise, you will configure Windows 10 using Windows 10 Settings and Control Panel.
Mindset	When you click the Settings option, you launch the Settings application that is based on the Modern UI interface to access common settings. In previous versions of Windows, the Control Panel was the primary graphical utility to configure the Windows environment and hardware devices.
Completion time	20 minutes

1. Log on to **LON-CL1** as **adatum\administrator** with the password of **Pa$$w0rd**.

2. Click the **Start** button and then click **Settings**. The Settings window opens as shown in Figure 4-1.

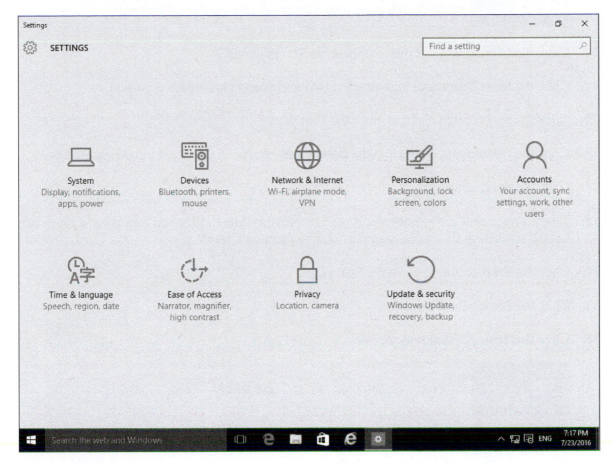

Figure 4-1
Windows 10 Settings

3. Click the **System** option.

4. Click the **Apps & features** option.

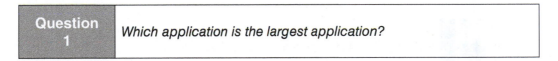

Question 1	Which application is the largest application?

5. Scroll down and click **Microsoft Solitaire Collection**. Then click **Uninstall**. Click **Uninstall** again.

6. Take a screen shot showing that the Microsoft Solitaire Collection has been removed by pressing **Alt+PrtScr** and then paste it into your Lab04_worksheet file in the page provided by pressing **Ctrl+V**.

7. Click the **back** button (left arrow at the top of the Settings window).

8. Click the **Personalization** option.

9. Click **Start**.

Question 2	When you click the Start button, does the start page take up the full screen? Why does it take up or not take up the full screen?

10. Click the **Choose which folders appear on Start** option.

11. Click the **Start** button and look to see if Documents and Downloads are listed.

12. Click the **Start** button again to close the Start page.

13. Click the **Documents** option and the **Downloads** option, so that the settings is set to **On**.

14. Click the **Start** button.

15. Take a screen shot showing the Start page by pressing **Alt+PrtScr** and then paste it into your Lab04_worksheet file in the page provided by pressing **Ctrl+V**.

16. Click the **Start** button to close the Start page.

17. Click the **Back** button twice.

18. Click **the Time & Language** option.

Question 3	Why can't you change the date and time?

19. Close the **Settings** window.

20. Right-click the **Start** button and choose **Control Panel**.

21. If the Control Panel is showing large or small icons, change the View by option to **Category**.

22. Click the **System and Security** options.

23. Click **System**.

Question 4	How much RAM does your system have?

24. At the top of the window, click **Control Panel**.

25. Under Hardware and Sound, click **View devices and printers**.

Question 5	How many printers are installed?

26. Close the Devices and Printers window.

Leave LON-CL1 open for the next exercise.

Exercise 4.2	Configuring Power Settings
Overview	In this exercise, you will create and manage a power plan.
Mindset	Power management is the balancing of power consumption with performance. Windows 10 includes extensive power management capabilities, including supporting the Advanced Configuration and Power Interface (ACPI), which can be configured using power plans. The power plans can be configured using the Control Panel Power Options, using Group Policy, or via the command prompt.
Completion time	15 minutes

1. On **LON-CL1**, right-click the **Start** button and choose **Control Panel**.

2. Click **Hardware and Sound > Power Options**. The Power Options page opens as shown in Figure 4-2.

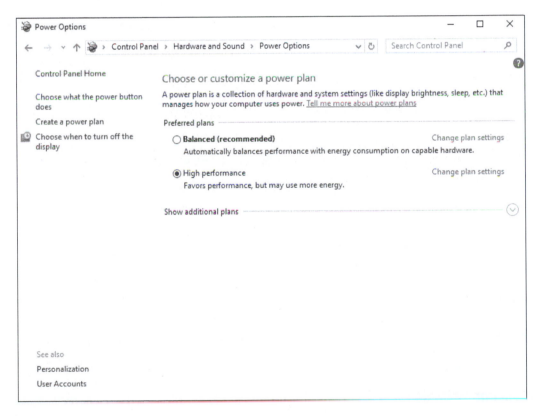

Figure 4-2
Managing Power Options

3. Click the **Choose what the power button does** option.

Question 6	By default, what happens when the power button is pressed?

4. Click the **Back** (left arrow) button.

Question 7	Which power plan is being used by the system?

5. Click the small down arrow next to **Show additional plans.**

Question 8	Which power plan was hidden?

6. Click the **Create a power plan** option.

7. In the Create a Power Plan Wizard, Balanced (recommended) is already selected. In the Plan name text box, type **MyPowerPlan** and then click **Next**.

8. On the Change Settings for the Plan page, click the **Create** button.

9. Take a screen shot of the Power Options page by pressing **Alt+PrtScr** and then paste it into your Lab04_worksheet file in the page provided by pressing **Ctrl+V**.

10. Next to MyPowerPlan, click **Change plan settings**.

11. Click **Change advanced power settings**. The Power Options dialog box opens.

Question 9	At what point is the hard disk turned off when it's not being used?

12. Change the Setting (Minutes) to **30**.

13. Take a screen shot of the Power Options dialog box by pressing **Alt+PrtScr** and then paste it into your Lab04_worksheet file in the page provided by pressing **Ctrl+V**.

14. Expand the **Wireless Adapter Settings** node and then expand the **Power Savings Mode** node.

Question 10	Which power saving mode for wireless adapters is the system set to?

15. Click **OK**.

16. Close the Edit Plan Settings window.

Leave LON-CL1 open for the exercise.

Exercise 4.3	Configuring Internet Explorer
Overview	In this exercise, you will configure various Internet Explorer options, including configuring security zones, Pop-up Blocker, add-ons, and compatibility mode.
Mindset	Internet Explorer is Microsoft's traditional browser, offering several features to protect your security and privacy while you browse the web, including phishing filters, Protected Mode, Pop-up Blocker, Add-on Manager, download files or software notification, and the use of digital signatures and 128-bit secure (SSL) connections when using secure websites.
Completion time	40 minutes

1. On LON-CL1, click the **Start** button and then type **IE**. From the search results, click **Internet Explorer Desktop app**. In the Set up Internet Explorer dialog box, select the **Use recommended security and compatibility settings** option and then click **OK**.

2. Using Internet Explorer, open **http://www.microsoft.com**. (Don't worry if you are not connected to the Internet.)

3. Click the **Tools** button (gear button) and then select **Internet options**.

4. In the Internet options dialog box (see Figure 4-3), in the Home page section, click the **Use current** button.

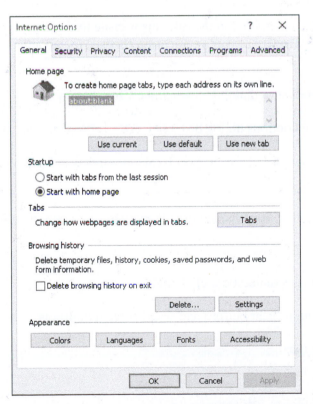

Figure 4-3
Configuring Internet Options

5. To clear your history, click the **Delete** button in the Browsing history section.

> | Question 11 | Which default options will be deleted? |
> | --- | --- |

6. With the default options already selected, click the **Delete** button.

7. Click the **Security** Tab.

8. Click the **Internet** zone.

9. Click the **Custom level** button.

> | Question 12 | When you click the Reset custom settings option, which level is the default? |
> | --- | --- |

> | Question 13 | Under ActiveX controls and plug-ins, which option is selected for Allow previously unused ActiveX controls to run without prompt? |
> | --- | --- |

10. To close the security settings for the Internet zone, click the **Cancel** button

11. Click **Trusted** sites.

12. Click the **Sites** button.

13. In the Trusted sites dialog box, in the Add this website to the zone, type **http://www.adatum.com**. Deselect the **Require server verification (https:) for all sites in this zone** option. Click **Add**.

14. To close the **Trusted** sites dialog box, click the **Close** button.

15. To close the Internet options dialog box, click **OK**.

16. Right-click the white part of the Internet Explorer window and choose **Properties**.

> | Question 14 | Which zone is assigned to http://www.microsoft.com? |
> | --- | --- |

17. To close the Properties dialog box, click **OK**.

18. Click the **Tools** button (gear button) and select **Internet options**.

19. Click the **Privacy** tab.

20. In the Pop-up Blocker section, click the **Settings** button.

21. In the Pop-up blocker Settings dialog box, in the Address of website to allow, type **www.micro-soft.com** and then click the **Add** button.

22. Take a screen shot of the Pop-up Blocker Settings dialog box by pressing **Alt+PrtScr** and then paste it into your Lab04_worksheet file in the page provided by pressing **Ctrl+V**.

23. To close the Pop-up blocking Settings dialog box, click the **Close** button

24. Click the **Connections** tab.

25. In the Local Area Network (LAN) settings section, click the **LAN settings** button.

26. If the Automatically detect settings option is selected, deselect the option.

27. Select **Use a proxy server for your LAN**.

28. In the Address text box, type **172.24.255.20** for the address. For the port text box, type **8080**. Select the **Bypass proxy server for local addresses** option.

29. Take a screen shot of the Local Area Network (LAN) Settings dialog box by pressing **Alt+PrtScr** and then paste it into your Lab04_worksheet file in the page provided by pressing **Ctrl+V**.

30. Click **OK** to close the Local Area Network (LAN) Settings dialog box and then click the **OK** button to close the Internet options dialog box.

31. Open the Internet options again and go back into the **Local Area Network (LAN) Settings** again to deselect the **Use a proxy server for your LAN** option. Select the **Automatically detect settings** option.

32. To close the Local Area Network (LAN) Settings dialog box, click the **OK** button.

33. Click the **Programs** tab.

34. Click the **Manage add-ons** button.

35. Review the Toolbars and Extensions, Search Providers, Accelerators and Tracking Protection to see your managed add-ons.

36. Close the Manage Add-ons dialog box.

37. To close the Internet Options dialog box, click **OK**.

38. Click the **Tools** button (gear button) and then select **Compatibility View settings**.

39. If you have a website that is not compatible with Internet Explorer 11, in the Add this website text box, type the website URL. For our example, type **www.adatum.com** and then click the **Add** button.

40. Take a screen shot of the Compatibility View Settings dialog box by pressing **Alt+PrtScr** and then paste the resulting image into the Lab04_worksheet file in the page provided by pressing **Ctrl+V**.

41. Click the **Close** button.

42. Click the **Tools** button (gear button) and select **Internet options**.

43. Click the **Advanced** tab.

44. Under the Browsing section, deselect **Show friendly HTTP error messages** option. Sometimes when you get an error message, it might benefit you to deselect this option so that you get a more meaningful error message.

45. Browse through the other options under the Advanced settings.

46. Click the **Reset** button. If you or an application made changes to Internet Explorer and you discover that Internet Explorer is unstable, you should click **Restore advanced settings** or click the **Reset** button.

47. When you are prompted to confirm that you want to reset all Internet Explorer settings, click the **Reset** button.

48. Take a screen shot of the Reset Internet Explorer Settings dialog box by pressing **Alt+PrtScr** and then paste the resulting image into the Lab04_worksheet file in the page provided by pressing **Ctrl+V**.

49. To close the Reset Internet Explorer Settings dialog box, click the **Close** button.

50. Close **Internet Explorer**.

Leave LON-CL1 open for the exercise.

Exercise 4.4	Installing Hyper-V
Overview	In this exercise, you will install the Hyper-V using DISM.
Mindset	Hyper-V enables you to create and manage virtual machines (VMs) using a virtual switch. These VMs can be used to test your applications for compatibility with new operating systems, allow you to run applications written for older versions of Windows, or isolate an application.
Completion time	10 minutes

1. On LON-CL1, right-click the **Start** button and choose **Command Prompt** (**Admin**).

2. Execute the following commands:

```
Dism /online /enable-feature /featurename:Microsoft-Hyper-V /All
```

NOTE	*On a physical computer running Windows 10, you can install Hyper-V using the Programs and Features. On a Hyper-V machine, you cannot run Hyper-V using the Program Features and you cannot run virtual machines. In other words, you can not run a Hyper-V virtual machine on another Hyper-V machine. However, you can install Hyper-V using DISM and you can create and manage virtual machines.*

3. When you are prompted to reboot, press the **y** key.

4. Log on to **LON-CL1** as **adatum\administrator** with the password of **Pa$$w0rd**.

5. Right-click the **Start** button and choose **Programs and Features**.

Question 15	*Where else can you find the Programs and Features?*

6. Click **Turn Windows features on or off**.

7. In the Windows Features dialog box, expand the **Hyper-V** node.

8. Take a screen shot of the Windows Features dialog box showing the Hyper-V is installed by pressing **Alt+PrtScr** and then paste it into your Lab04_worksheet file in the page provided by pressing **Ctrl+V**.

9. Close the Windows Features dialog box and then close Control Panel.

Leave LON-CL1 open for the next exercise.

Exercise 4.5	Creating and Managing Virtual Machines
Overview	In this exercise, you will create a virtual machine.
Mindset	A virtual machine (VM) is a self-contained, isolated unit that can be easily moved from one physical computer to another, runs its own operating system, and includes its own virtual hardware configuration. After you have installed Hyper-V, you can then use the Hyper-V Manager console to create and manage VMs.
Completion time	30 minutes

1. On LON-CL1, right-click the **Start** button and choose **Control Panel**.

2. In the Search Control Panel text box, type **Administrative Tools**. Then from the search results, click **Administrative Tools**.

3. When Administrative Tools opens, double-click **Hyper-V Manager**. Hyper-V Manager opens as shown in Figure 4-4.

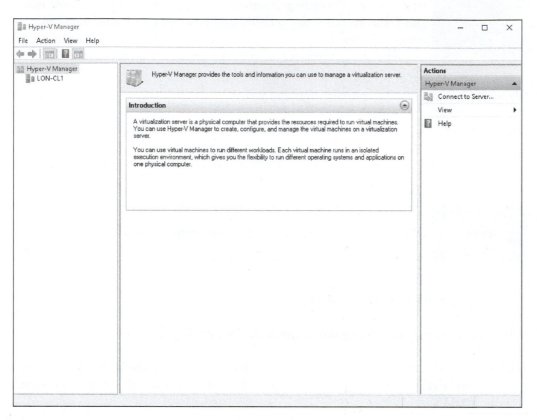

Figure 4-4
The Hyper-V Manager

4. Right-click **LON-CL1** and choose **New > Virtual Machine**.

5. In the New Virtual Machine Wizard, on the Before You Begin page, click **Next**.

6. On the Specify Name and Location page, in the Name text box, type **VM1**.

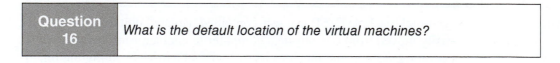

| Question 16 | *What is the default location of the virtual machines?* |

7. Click **Next**.

8. On the Specify Generation page, Generation 1 is already selected. Click **Next**.

9. On the Assign Memory page, answer the following question. Then in the Startup memory box, type **2048**. Click **Next**.

Question 17	*What is the default startup memory?*

10. Normally, you would select a virtual switch. However, because a virtual switch is not configured yet, on the Configuring Networking page, click **Next.**

11. On the Connect Virtual Hard Disk page, change the size to **20** GB. Click **Next**.

12. On the Installation Options page, for the purposes of our lab environment, click **Next**.

13. On the Summary page, click **Finish**.

14. In Hyper-V Manager, click **LON-CL1**.

15. Take a screen shot of Hyper-V Manager showing the new VM by pressing **Alt+PrtScr** and then paste it into your Lab04_worksheet file in the page provided by pressing **Ctrl+V**.

16. Right-click **VM1** and choose **Settings**.

17. Click **Memory**.

18. Change the Minimum RAM setting to **1024** MB.

19. Click **Processor**.

20. Change the number of virtual processors from 1 to **2**.

21. Take a screen shot of Hyper-V Manager showing the Processor setting by pressing **Alt+PrtScr** and then paste it into your Lab04_worksheet file in the page provided by pressing **Ctrl+V**.

22. To close the Settings window, click the **OK** button.

23. On LON-CL1, using Hyper-V Manager, under Actions, click **Virtual Switch Manager**. The Virtual Switch Manager dialog box opens, as shown in Figure 4-5.

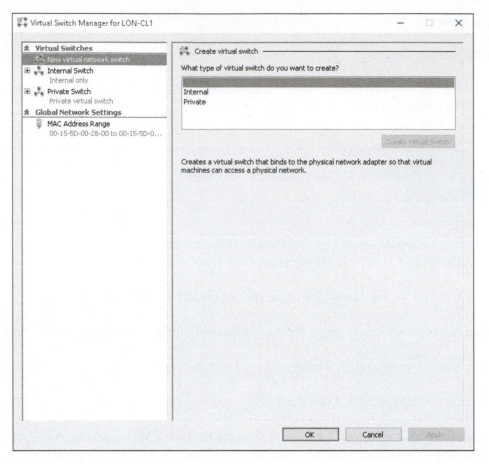

Figure 4-5
Managing virtual switches

24. When you are prompted to choose the type of virtual switch you want to create, select **Private** and then click the **Create Virtual Switch** button.

25. In the Name text box, type **Private Switch** and then click **Apply**.

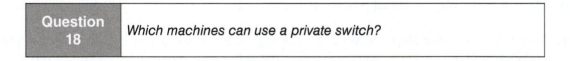

Question 18	*Which machines can use a private switch?*

26. Take a screen shot of Virtual Switch Manager by pressing **Alt+PrtScr** and then paste it into your Lab04_worksheet file in the page provided by pressing **Ctrl+V**.

27. Click **New virtual network switch**.

28. When you are prompted to choose the type of virtual switch to create, click **Internal** and then click **Create Virtual Switch**.

29. In the Name text box, type **Internal Switch** and then click **Apply**.

30. Take a screen shot of Virtual Switch Manager by pressing **Alt+PrtScr** and then paste it into your Lab04_worksheet file in the page provided by pressing **Ctrl+V**.

31. Click **OK** to close the Virtual Switch Manager.

32. On Hyper-V Manager, using Hyper-V Manager, right-click **VM1** and choose **Settings**.

33. In the Settings dialog box, click the **Network Adapter** vertical tab, as shown in Figure 4-6.

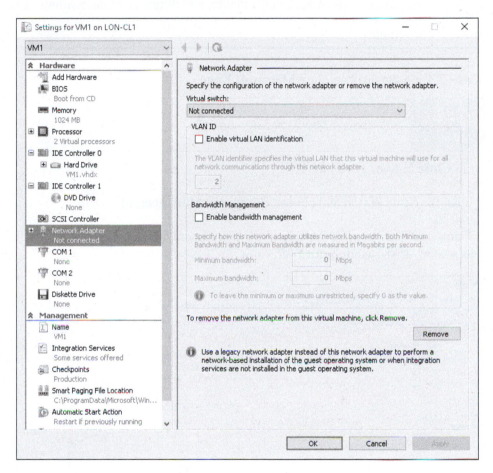

Figure 4-6
Managing network adapters

34. On the Network Adapter page, for the Virtual switch option, click the down arrow and select **Private Switch**.

35. Take a screen shot of Settings window by pressing **Alt+PrtScr** and then paste it into your Lab04_worksheet file in the page provided by pressing **Ctrl+V**.

36. Click **OK** to close the Settings dialog box.

Remain logged in to LON-CL1 but close Hyper-V Manager and Administrative Tools.

Lab Challenge	Configuring Microsoft Edge
Overview	In this exercise, you will configure the available Microsoft Edge settings.
Mindset	Microsoft Edge is Microsoft's new lightweight web browser with a layout engine built around web standards designed to replace Internet Explorer as the default web browser. It integrates with Cortana, annotation tools, Adobe Flash Player, a PDF reader, and a reading mode.
Completion time	10 minutes

1. On LON-CL1, on the taskbar, click **Microsoft Edge**.

Question 19	Why doesn't Microsoft Edge open?

2. Click the **Close** button.

3. Right-click the **Start** button and choose **Computer Management**.

4. In the Computer Management console, expand the **Local Users and Groups** node and then click the **Users** node, as shown in Figure 4-7.

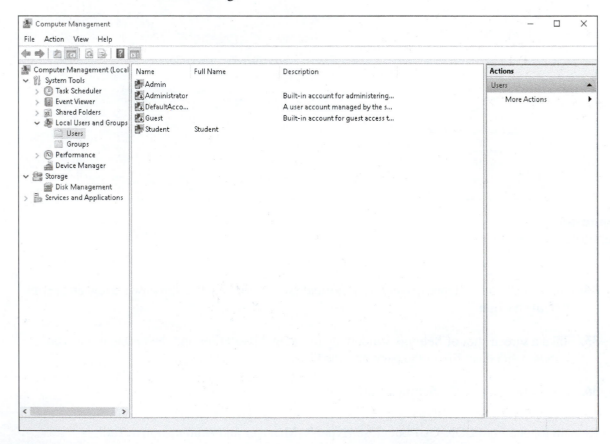

Figure 4-7
Managing local user accounts

5. Right-click the **Users** node and choose **New User**.

6. In the New User dialog box, type the following information:

   User name: **JSmith**

   Full Name: **John Smith**

   Password and Confirm password: **Pa$$w0rd**

7. Deselect the **User must change password at next logon** option and then click the **Create** button.

8. Click the **Close** button to close the New User dialog box.

9. Take a screen shot showing the Computer Management console showing the new user by pressing **Alt+PrtScr** and then paste it into your Lab04_worksheet file in the page provided by pressing **Ctrl+V**.

10. Double-click the **JSmith** account.

11. In the JSmith Properties dialog box, click the **Member Of** tab.

Question 20	What group is JSmith member of?

12. Click the **Add** button.

13. In the Select Groups dialog box, answer the following question, and then in the Enter the object names to select text box, type **Administrators** and click **OK**.

Question 21	Which location will the group come from based on the From this location field?

14. To close the JSmith Properties dialog box, click **OK**.

15. Click the **Start** button. Then click **Administrator** and click **Sign out**.

16. Log on by clicking **Other user**, then log on as **LON-CL1\JSmith** with the password of **Pa$$w0rd**. It will take a couple of minutes to create the user profile.

17. On the taskbar, click the **Microsoft Edge** icon.

18. Click the **. . .** button and then click **Settings**.

19. Click the **View favorites settings** button.

20. Change the Show the favorite bar from Off to **On**.

21. Take a screen shot of the Can't reach this page window by pressing **Alt+PrtScr** and then paste it into your Lab04_worksheet file in the page provided by pressing **Ctrl+V**.

22. Click the back button (<<).

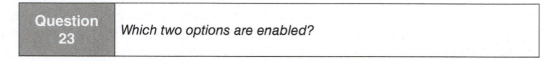

Question 22	What is the reading view stytle and the font size?

23. Click **View advanced settings**.

Question 23	Which two options are enabled?

24. Scroll down and look at the available options.

25. Close **Microsoft Edge**.

26. Close all Windows and log off LON-CL1.

End of lab.

LAB 5

IMPLEMENTING WINDOWS IN AN ENTERPRISE ENVIRONMENT

THIS LAB CONTAINS THE FOLLOWING EXERCISES AND ACTIVITIES:

Exercise 5.1 Installing the Windows Assessment and Deployment Kit

Exercise 5.2 Creating a Provisioning Package with the Windows Imaging and Configuration Design Tool

Exercise 5.3 Configuring Group Policy

Lab Challenge Configuring User Account Control (UAC)

BEFORE YOU BEGIN

The lab environment consists of student workstations connected to a local area network, along with a server that functions as the domain controller for a domain called adatum.com. The computers required for this lab are listed in Table 5-1.

Table 5-1
Computers required for Lab 5

Computer	Operating System	Computer Name
Server (VM 1)	Windows Server 2012 R2	LON-DC1
Server (VM 2)	Windows Server 2012 R2	LON-SRV2
Client (VM 3)	Windows 10	LON-CL1

In addition to the computers, you will also require the software listed in Table 5-2 to complete Lab 5.

Table 5-2
Software required for Lab 5

Software	Location
Windows Assessment and Deployment Kit (ADK) for Windows 10	\\LON-DC1\Software
Lab 5 student worksheet	Lab05_worksheet.docx (provided by instructor)

Working with Lab Worksheets

Each lab in this manual requires that you answer questions, shoot screen shots, and perform other activities that you will document in a worksheet named for the lab, such as Lab05_worksheet.docx. You will find these worksheets on the book companion site. It is recommended that you use a USB flash drive to store your worksheets, so you can submit them to your instructor for review. As you perform the exercises in each lab, open the appropriate worksheet file, fill in the required information, and then save the file to your flash drive.

SCENARIO

After completing this lab, you will be able to:

■ Install the Windows Assessment and Deployment Kit

■ Create a provisioning package with the Windows Imaging and Configuration Design Tool

■ Configure Group Policy

■ Configure User Account Control (UAC)

Estimated lab time: 60 minutes

Exercise 5.1	Installing the Windows Assessment and Deployment Kit
Overview	In this exercise, you will install the Windows Assessment and Deployment Kit, which includes the Windows Imaging and Configuration Designer Tool
Mindset	With larger companies, adopting a new desktop operating system is inherently much more difficult due to wider application incompatibility, the need for more user training, and greater complexity of deployment. To help with application compatibility and Windows deployment, Microsoft developed the Windows Assessment and Deployment Kit (ADK) for Windows 10.
Completion time	20 minutes

1. Log on to **LON-SVR2** as **adatum\administrator** with the password of the **Pa$$w0rd**.

2. Launch **File Explorer** and then open the **\\LON-DC1\software** folder. Then double-click **adksetup**. If you are prompted to confirm that you want to run the file, click **Run**.

3. On the Specify Location page, click **Next**.

4. On the Windows Kits Privacy page, click **Next**.

5. On the License Agreement page, click **Accept**.

6. On the Select the features you want to install page (as shown in Figure 5-1), click **Install**.

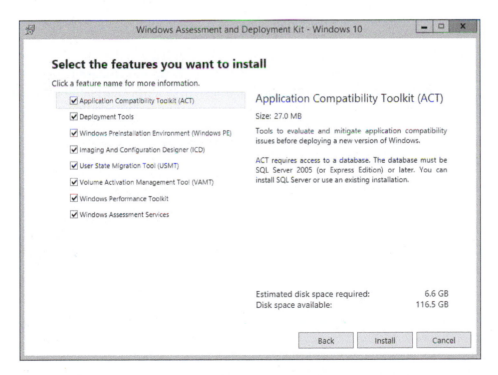

Figure 5-1
Selecting Windows ADK features

7. Take a screen shot of the Welcome to the Windows Assessment and Deployment Kit — Windows 10! screen by pressing **Alt+PrtScr** and then paste it into your Lab05_worksheet file in the page provided by pressing **Ctrl+V**.

8. Click **Close**.

Leave LON-SRVR2 logged in for the next exercise.

Exercise 5.2	Creating a Provisioning Package with the Windows Imaging and Configuration Designer Tool
Overview	In this exercise, you will create a provioning package using the Windows Imaging and Configuration Designer Tool that will be used to configure systems running Windows 10.
Mindset	The Imaging and Configuration Designer (ICD) helps you create or modify provisioning packages to update an image without deploying the image, making the changes on a new master system, and re-capturing the image. ICD can also be used to create provisioning packages (*.ppkg), which are small executable programs that prepare one or more devices for corporate use. You can use it to deploy an operating system to computers or you can use it to modify computer systems, such as connecting to a Wi-Fi network, adding certificates, connecting to an Active Directory domain, setting user rights, customizing the start menu, upgrading editions of Windows, or enrolling a device to Mobile Device Management (MDM).
Completion time	20 minutes

1. On LON-SRV2, click **Start** and then click **All apps**. Scroll down the list, select and expand **Windows Kits,** and then scroll down to and then click **Windows Imaging and Configuration Designer**. If you are prompted to confirm that you want to allow this app to make changes to your PC, click **Yes**.

2. On the Windows Imaging and Configuration Designer page (see Figure 5-2), click the **New provisioning package** icon.

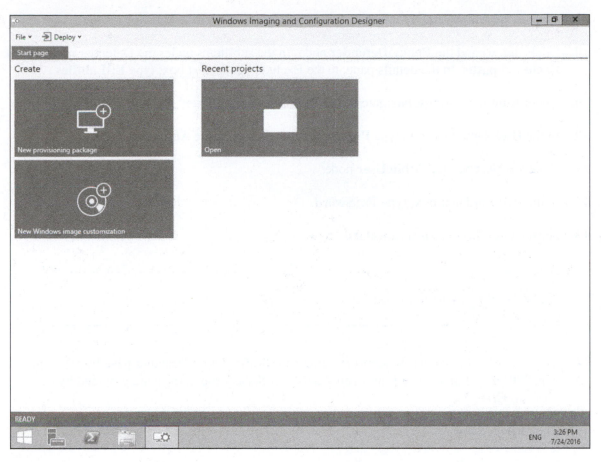

Figure 5-2
Opening Windows Imaging and Configuration Designer

3. When the New Project Wizard starts, on the Enter project details page, in the Name text box as well as in the Description text box, type **Project01**. Click **Next**.

4. On the Choose which settings to view and configure page, select **Common to all Windows desktop editions** and then click **Next**.

5. On the Import a provisioning package page, click **Finish**.

6. On the Project01 tab, with the view set to All settings, under Runtime, select and expand **Policies**. Then navigate to and click **Policies > Camera > AllowCamera**.

NOTE	Sometimes, Windows Imaging and Configuration Designer is slow to respond. If so, click on an option and be patient for ICD to respond. If a message displays, indicating ICD.exe is not responding, click Wait for the program to respond.

7. Change the AllowCamera option from **NOT CONFIGURED** to **Yes**.

8. Click and expand the **Policy\Defender** node. In the sub-items under the Defender node, select **Excluded paths**. In the details pane, in the Excluded paths text box, type **E:\Labfiles**.

9. Under Runtime settings, navigate to and click **Accounts > User**.

10. In the UserName text box, type **PublicUser** and then click the **Add** button.

11. Click the **UserName: PublicUser** node.

12. In the Password text box, type **Pa$$w0rd**.

13. For the UserGroup, select **Standard Users**.

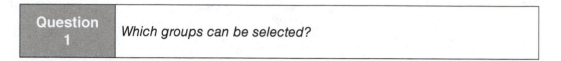

Question 1	Which groups can be selected?

14. Take a screen shot of the Windows Imaging and Configuration Designer page by pressing **Alt+PrtScr** and then paste it into your Lab05_worksheet file in the page provided by pressing **Ctrl+V**.

15. Click **File > Save**.

16. Click **Export > Provisioning package**.

17. In the Build window, in the Owner drop-down list, change the value from **OEM** to **IT Admin** and then click **Next**.

18. On the Select security details for the provisioning package page, deselect the **Encrypt package** option and then click **Next**.

19. On the Select where to save the provisioning package page, in the Select where to save the provisioning package text box, type **\\LON-DC1\Software\Project01.ppkg** and then click **Next**.

20. On the Build the provisioning package page, click **Build**.

21. When the package is built, click **Finish**.

22. Log on to **LON-CL1** as **adatum\administrator** with the password of the **Pa$$w0rd**.

23. Open File Explorer by clicking the **File Explorer** icon on the taskbar.

24. Using File Explorer, open **\\LON-DC1\Software**.

25. Double-click the **Project01.ppkg** file.

26. When you are prompted to confirm that you trust the package source, click **Yes, add it**.

Leave LON-CL1 logged in for the next exercise. Log off LON-SVR2.

Exercise 5.3	Configuring Group Policy
Overview	In this exercise, you will create a Group Policy Object that will specify the background image for a client running the Windows operating system.
Mindset	Group Policy is one of the most powerful features of Active Directory; it controls the working environment for user accounts and computer accounts. Group Policy provides centralized management and configuration of operating systems, applications, and user settings in an Active Directory environment. A Group Policy Object (GPO) is a collection of those user and computer settings.
Completion time	10 minutes

1. Log on to **LON-DC1** as **adatum\administrator** with the password of **Pa$$w0rd**.

2. In Server Manager, click **Tools > Group Policy Management**.

3. In the Group Policy Management window (see Figure 5-3), navigate to and click **Forest: Adatum.com\Domains\Adatum.com\Sales**.

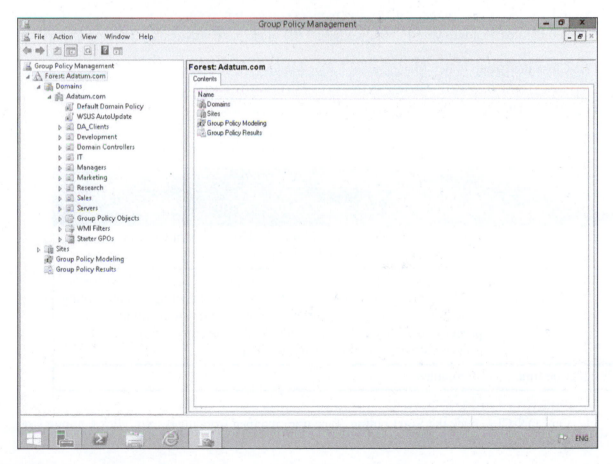

Figure 5-3
Opening Group Policy Management

4. Right-click the **Sales** node and choose **Create a GPO in this domain, and Link it here**.

5. In the New GPO dialog box, in the Name text box, type **Desktop** and then click **OK**.

6. Right-click the **Desktop** GPO and choose **Edit.**

7. Navigate to **User Configuration\Policies\Administrative Templates\Desktop\Desktop**.

8. Double-click **Desktop Wallpaper**.

9. In the Desktop Wallpaper dialog box, click **Enabled**.

10. In the Wallpaper Name text box, type **C:\Windows\Web\Screen\img104.jpg**.

Question 2	*What is the wallpaper style set to?*

11. Click **OK** to close the Desktop Wallpaper dialog box.

12. Take a screen shot showing the Group Policy Manager Editor window by pressing **Alt+PrtScr** and then paste it into your Lab05_worksheet file in the page provided by pressing **Ctrl+V**.

13. Close the Group Policy Management Editor window.

Leave LON-DC1 and LON-CL1 open for the next exercise.

Lab Challenge	Configuring User Account Control (UAC)
Overview	In this exercise, you will configure the User Account Control settings using the Control Panel and a Group Policy Object.
Mindset	User Access Control (UAC) is a technology used with Windows Vista, 7, 8/8.1, and 10 to enhance system security by detecting and preventing unauthorized changes to the system. Some applications might not run properly using a standard user credential if the application needs to access restricted files or registry location.
Completion time	10 minutes

1. On LON-CL1, click the **Start** button. Type **uac**, and then from the results, click **Change User Account Control settings**.

2. In the User Account Control Settings box (see Figure 5-4), slide the slider down one notch.

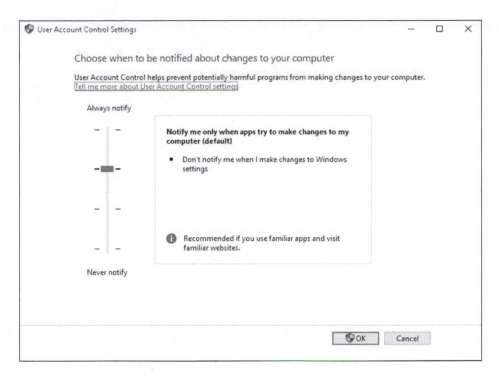

Figure 5-4
Configuring User Account Control Settings

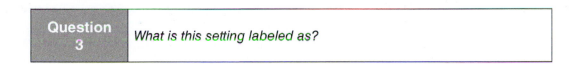

Question 3	What is this setting labeled as?

3. Close the User Account Control Settings window by clicking **OK**.

4. On LON-CL1, click the **Start** button. Type **secpol.msc**, and then from Results, choose **secpol.msc**.

5. In the Local Security Policy console, expand **Local Policies** and then click **Security Options**.

6. Scroll down to the bottom of the policy list until you see the ten policies with the User Account Control prefix.

Question 4	Which setting is User Account Control: Behavior of the elevation prompt for standards users set to?

7. Double-click the **User Account Control: Behavior of the elevation prompt for administrators in Admin Approval mode** setting.

8. On the Local Security Setting tab, click the drop-down arrow, choose **Elevate without prompting**, and then click **OK**.

9. Take a screen shot showing the Group Policy Manager Editor window by pressing **Alt+PrtScr** and then paste it into your Lab05_worksheet file in the page provided by pressing **Ctrl+V**.

End of lab.

LAB 6
CONFIGURING NETWORKING

THIS LAB CONTAINS THE FOLLOWING EXERCISES AND ACTIVITIES:

Exercise 6.1	Configuring IPv4 Settings
Exercise 6.2	Configuring IPv6 Settings
Exercise 6.3	Configuring Advanced Shared Settings for Network Locations
Exercise 6.4	Configuring Windows Firewall
Exercise 6.5	Configuring a VPN Client
Lab Challenge	Configuring Wi-Fi Networking

BEFORE YOU BEGIN

The lab environment consists of student workstations connected to a local area network, along with a server that functions as the domain controller for a domain called adatum.com. The computers required for this lab are listed in Table 6-1.

Table 6-1
Computers required for Lab 6

Computer	Operating System	Computer Name
Server (VM 1)	Windows Server 2012 R2	LON-DC1
Server (VM 2)	Windows Server 2012 R2	LON-RTR
Client (VM 3)	Windows 10	LON-CL1

In addition to the computers, you will also require the software listed in Table 6-2 to complete Lab 6.

Table 6-2
Software required for Lab 6

Software	Location
Lab 6 student worksheet	Lab06_worksheet.docx (provided by instructor)

Working with Lab Worksheets

Each lab in this manual requires that you answer questions, shoot screen shots, and perform other activities that you will document in a worksheet named for the lab, such as Lab06_worksheet.docx. You will find these worksheets on the book companion site. It is recommended that you use a USB flash drive to store your worksheets, so you can submit them to your instructor for review. As you perform the exercises in each lab, open the appropriate worksheet file using WordPad, fill in the required information, and save the file to your flash drive.

SCENARIO

After completing this lab, you will be able to:

■ Configure IPv4 and IPv6 settings

■ Configure Advanced Shared Settings for network locations

■ Configure Windows Firewall

■ Configure a VPN client

■ Configure Wi-Fi Networking

Estimated lab time: 95 minutes

Exercise 6.1	Configuring IPv4 Settings
Overview	In this exercise, you will configure IPv4 settings, including enabling a DHCP address and manually configuring the IPv4 settings.
Mindset	Network settings can be configured either manually or automatically using DHCP. When using manual settings, you can unknowingly introduce configuration issues that can affect communications. Using a centralized approach to IP address management requires you to have a solid understanding of DHCP.
Completion time	20 minutes

1. Log on to **LON-CL1** as **adatum\administrator** with the password of **Pa$$w0rd**.

2. On **LON-CL1**, right-click the **Network Status** icon and choose **Open Network and Sharing Center**. The Network and Sharing Center page opens as shown in Figure 6-1.

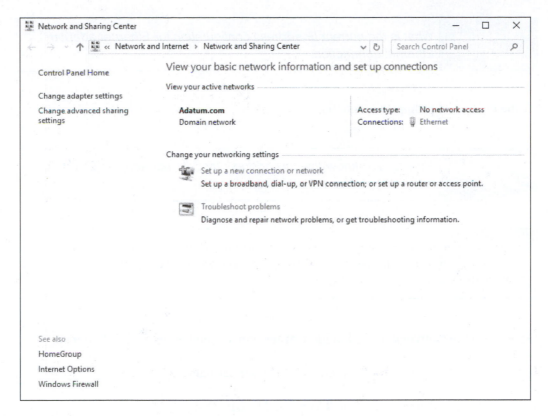

Figure 6-1
The Network and Sharing Center page

3. On the Network and Sharing Center page, click **Change adapter settings**.

4. Double-click the first **Ethernet** connection.

5. In the Ethernet Status dialog box, click **Properties**.

6. In the Ethernet Properties dialog box, scroll down and double-click **Internet Protocol Version 4 (TCP/IPv4)**.

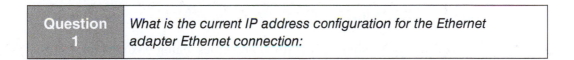

Question 1	*What is the current IP address configuration for the Ethernet adapter Ethernet connection:*

7. Select the **Obtain an IP address automatically** option. Then Select the **Obtain DNS server address automatically** option. Click **OK**.

8. Close the Ethernet Properties dialog box by clicking **OK**.

9. Close the Ethernet Status dialog box by clicking **Close**.

10. Right-click the **Start** button and choose **Command Prompt** (**Admin**).

11. At the command prompt, execute the `ipconfig` command.

Question 2	What is the current IP address configuration for Ethernet adapter Ethernet connection:

12. At the command prompt, execute the `ipconfig /all` command.

Question 3	How do you know that this address for Ethernet adapter Ethernet was assigned by a DHCP server?

Question 4	The default gateway could be assigned to any local IP address. Which address range could you assign to the Default gateway to indicate a local router?

13. Go back to the **Network and Sharing Center** window and double-click **Ethernet**.

14. In the Ethernet Status dialog box, click the **Properties** button.

15. Double-click the **Internet Protocol Version 4 (TCP/IPv4)**.

16. In the Internet Protocol Version 4 (TCP/IPv4) Properties dialog box, select **Use the following IP address**.

17. Specify the following information:

    IP address: **172.16.0.40**

    Subnet mask: **255.255.0.0**

    Default gateway: **172.16.0.1**

18. Select the Use the following DNS server addresses option.

    Preferred DNS server: **172.16.0.10**

19. Close the Internet Protocol Version 4 (TCP/IPv4) Properties dialog box by clicking **OK**.

20. Close the Ethernet Properties dialog box by clicking **OK**.

21. Close the Ethernet Status dialog box by clicking **Close**.

22. Go back to the command prompt window and execute the `ipconfig` command:

23. Take a screen shot of the Command Prompt window by pressing **Alt+PrtScr** and then paste it into your Lab06_worksheet file in the page provided by pressing **Ctrl+V**.

Leave the Command Prompt window open and leave the Network and Sharing Center open for the next exercise.

Exercise 6.2	Configuring IPv6 Settings
Overview	In this exercise, you will configure IPv6 settings.
Mindset	To overcome this problem of running out of IPv4 addresses, as well as a few others, IPv6 was developed as the next-generation Internet Protocol version. Because IPv6 uses 128 bits, the addresses are usually divided into groups of 16 bits, written as 4 hex digits.
Completion time	10 minutes

1. On **LON-CL1**, using Network and Sharing Center, click **Ethernet**.

2. In the Ethernet Properties dialog box, click the **Details** button.

3. In the Network connections Details dialog box, answer the following question and then click **Close**.

Question 5	What is the Link-local IPv6 address?

4. In the Ethernet Status dialog box, click the **Properties** button.

5. In the **Properties** dialog box, scroll down and double-click **Internet Protocol Version 6 (TCP/IPv6)**, as shown in Figure 6-2. The Internet Protocol Version 6 (TCP/IPv6) Properties dialog box opens.

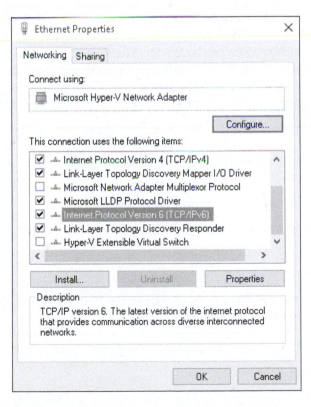

Figure 6-2
Opening Internet Protocol Version 6 (TCP/IPv6) properties

6. Select **Use the following IPv6 address**.

7. Type the following and then click **OK**.

   IPv6 address: **fe80:0:ac4a:aa04:713a:0:0:ce2b**

   Subnet prefix length: **64**

8. Close the Ethernet Properties dialog box by clicking **OK**.

9. Close the Ethernet Status dialog box by clicking **Close**.

10. Go back to the command window and execute the `ipconfig` command.

11. Take a screen shot of the Command Prompt window by pressing **Alt+PrtScr** and then paste it into your Lab06_worksheet file in the page provided by pressing **Ctrl+V**.

Close the Command Prompt window but leave the Network and Sharing Center open for the next exercise.

Exercise 6.3	Configuring Advanced Shared Settings for Network Locations
Overview	In this exercise, you will configure the Advanced Shared Settings for network locations.
Mindset	Windows 10 includes advanced sharing settings that allow you to configure network sharing settings based on your network location. Network profiles can be Private, Guest or Public, or All Networks. Each network profile features different defaults and these defaults are applied when connecting to and selecting a network connection.
Completion time	10 minutes

1. On **LON-CL1**, using the Network and Sharing Center, answer the following questions:

Question 6	*Which type of network location is the Ethernet connection using?*

Question 7	*When you have a second Ethernet adapter, which network location is used by the adapter?*

2. Click **Change advanced sharing settings**. The Advanced Sharing Settings page is shown in Figure 6-3.

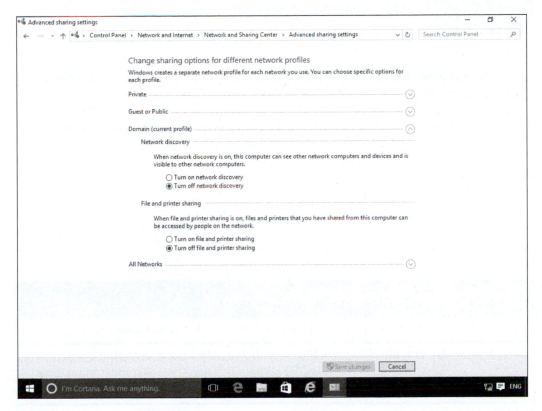

Figure 6-3
Configuring advanced sharing settings

3. Click the down arrow next to Domain.

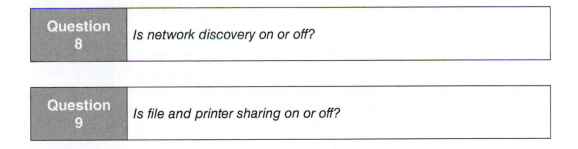

Question 8	Is network discovery on or off?

Question 9	Is file and printer sharing on or off?

4. Click the down arrow for All Networks.

Question 10	Is public folder sharing on or off?

5. Select the **Turn on sharing so anyone with network access can read and write files in the Public folders** option.

6. Take a screen shot of the Advanced Sharing Settings page by pressing **Alt+PrtScr** and then paste it into your Lab06_worksheet file in the page provided by pressing **Ctrl+V**.

7. Click **Save changes**.

Close the Network and Sharing Center window.

Exercise 6.4	Configuring Windows Firewall
Overview	In this exercise, you will create a Windows Firewall outbound rule.
Mindset	By default, Windows Firewall allows only certain outgoing packets to be sent from a Windows 10 computer. Therefore, you must know how to adjust the firewall to allow additional outgoing packets as needed.
Completion time	10 minutes

1. Log on to **LON-CL1** as **adatum\administrator** with the password of **Pa$$w0rd**.

2. On **LON-CL1**, right-click the **Start** button and choose **Control Panel**.

3. In Control Panel, click **System and Security** and then click **Windows Firewall**.

Question 11	You just installed a new application but users cannot connect to the application remotely. Which feature should be checked to ensure it's not preventing users from accessing a remote application?

4. On the Windows Firewall page (see Figure 6-4), in the left pane, click **Advanced settings**.

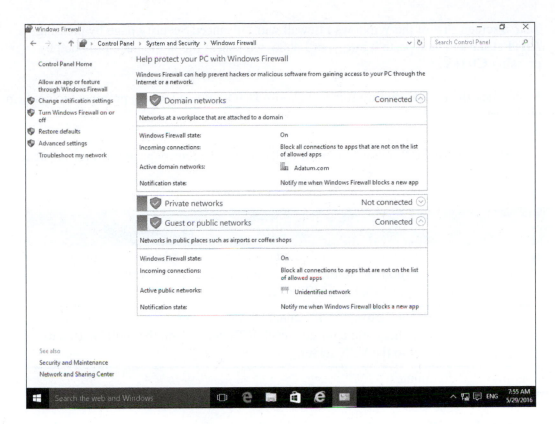

Figure 6-4
The Windows Firewall page

5. Click, then right-click **Outbound Rules**. Choose **New Rule**.

6. Select **Program** and then click **Next**.

7. Click **Browse** and then navigate to the location of your installation of Internet Explorer. This can usually be found at C:\Program Files\Internet Explorer\iexplore.exe. Click **iexplore.exe** and then click **Open**.

8. On the New Outbound Rule Wizard page, click **Next**.

9. Select **Block the connection** and then click **Next**.

10. Select **Domain, Private, and Public** and then click **Next**.

11. For the name of the profile, type **IE Restriction**; for the description, type **Restricts IE from connecting to the Internet**.

12. Click **Finish**.

13. Take a screen shot of the Windows Firewall with Advanced Security page by pressing **Alt+PrtScr** and then paste it into your Lab06_worksheet file in the page provided by pressing **Ctrl+V**.

14. Right-click the **IE Restriction** rule and choose **Delete**. When you are prompted to confirm, click **Yes**.

End of exercise. Leave the Windows Firewall with Advanced Security page open for the next exercise.

Exercise 6.5	Configuring a VPN Client
Overview	Now that you have configured the VPN server, you need to configure a client to connect to the VPN server. In this exercise, you will use LON_CL1 to act as a VPN client.
Mindset	When configuring a VPN client after the server is created, you must go to each client and configure each VPN connection that will be used to connect to the VPN server.
Completion time	20 minutes

1. Log on to **LON-DC1** using the **adatum\administrator** account with the password of **Pa$$w0rd**.

2. On Server Manager, click **Tools > Active Directory Users and Computers**.

3. Expand **adatum.com**, if needed, and then click **Users**.

4. Right-click the **Users** node and choose **New > User**.

5. In the New Object – User wizard, provide the following information and then click **Next**:

   First name: **Clark**

   Last name: **Wayne**

   Full name: **Clark Wayne**

   User logon name: **CWayne**

6. In the Password text box and the Confirm password text box, type **Pa$$w0rd**.

7. Deselect the **User must change password at next logon** option. Click **Next**.

8. Click **Finish**.

9. Double-click the **Clark Wayne** account. The Clark Wayne Properties dialog box opens.

10. Click the **Member Of** tab.

11. Click the **Add** button. In the Select Groups dialog box, type **Domain Admins**.

12. Click the **Dial-in** tab.

Question 12	What is the default setting for Network Access Permission?

13. In the Network Access Permission section, click to select **Allow access**.

14. Take a screen shot of the Administrator Properties window by pressing **Alt+PrtScr** and then paste it into your Lab06 worksheet file in the page provided by pressing **Ctrl+V**.

15. Close the Clark Wayne Properties dialog box by clicking **OK**.

16. Log on to **LON-CL1** using the **adatum\CWayne** account with the password of **Pa$$w0rd**. (It will take a couple minutes to create the CWayne profile.)

17. On LON-CL1, right-click the **Network Status** icon and choose **Open Network and Sharing Center**.

18. On the Network and Sharing Center page, choose **Set up a new connection or network**.

19. On the Set Up a Connection or Network page, choose **Connect to a workplace** and then click **Next**.

20. On the Connect to a Workplace page, click **Use my Internet connection (VPN)**.

21. If you are prompted to set up an Internet connection, click **I'll set up an Internet connection later**.

22. When you are prompted to type the Internet address to connect to, in the Internet address text box, type **172.16.0.13** and then click **Create**.

23. Click the **Network Status** icon (as shown in Figure 6-5) and click **VPN Connection**. When the Settings window opens, click **VPN Connection** and then click **Connect**.

Figure 6-5
Clicking a VPN Connection

24. Log on using the **Adatum\CWayne** and **Pa$$w0rd** password. A minute or two might pass before you are connected.

25. Take a screen shot of the Settings window showing a successful connection by pressing **Alt+PrtScr** and then paste it into your Lab06_worksheet file in the page provided by pressing **Ctrl+V**.

Question 13	A user cannot connect to the VPN server from home. Since the user will connect over the Internet, what is the first thing that you should check that the user should be able to do?

26. Click **VPN Connection** and then click **Disconnect**.

Log off LON-CL1.

Lab Challenge	Configuring Wi-Fi Networking
Overview	In this exercise, you will configure Wi-Fi on a physical computer running Windows 10.
Mindset	Because wireless technology sends radio waves into the open, anyone can capture data within the range of the antennas. Therefore, you need to implement encryption and other security measures to prevent data from being read over wireless technology.
Completion time	25 minutes

NOTE	*To perform this exercise, you must use a physical laptop or desktop with a wireless network card running Windows 10.*

1. Turn on the workstation and log on using the **adatum\administrator** account and the password **Pa$$w0rd** (or any other credentials provided by your instructor).

2. Right-click the **Start** button and choose **Control Panel**. The Control Panel window appears.

3. Click **Network and Internet** > **Network and Sharing Center**. The Network and Sharing Center page appears.

4. Click **Change adapter settings**.

5. If the Wireless Network Connection is disabled, right-click the connection and choose **Enable**.

Question 14	*The laptop has a built-in wireless adapter or the wireless adapter is physically installed on a computer and it does not appear in Network Connections. What is most likely the problem when it does not show in Network Connections?*

6. Right-click the **Wireless Network Connection** and choose **Properties**.

Question 15	*Which type of wireless network adapter do you have?*

7. Right-click **Wireless Network Connection** and choose **Connect/Disconnect**.

Question 16	Which wireless connections are being broadcasted as available?

Question 17	If you are using a laptop computer and you are expecting to see a wireless connection being broadcast but none are being displayed, what should you check first?

NOTE	Some OEM mobile computers might also have hot keys or software components that allow you to turn on or off the wireless radio.

8. Click **Open Network and Sharing Center**.

9. Click **Manage wireless networks**.

10. Click the **Add** button.

11. When it you are prompted to select how to add a network, click the **Manually create a network profile** option.

12. For the **Network name**, type **Adatum01** (or other name provided by your instructor). For the Security type, select **WPA2-Personal**. For the security key, type **Pa$$w0rd**.

Question 18	By default, which Encryption Type is used for WPA2?

13. Deselect the **Start this connection automatically** and select **Connect even if the network is not broadcasting**. Click the **Next** button.

14. Click the **Close** button.

15. Go back to the **Manage Wireless Networks**. You should notice the Adatum connection.

16. Go back to the **Network Connections** and then right-click **Wireless Network Connection** and choose **Connect/Disconnect**.

17. Click **Adatum01** and then click **Connect**.

18. Open a command prompt and execute the `ipconfig` command.

19. Execute a command to ping the default gateway. For example, if your gateway is 192.168.1.1, you would execute the `ping 192.168.1.1` command.

20. Back at the **Network Connections**, right-click **Wireless Network Connection** and choose **Status**.

Question 19	What is the SSID?
	What is the speed?
	What is the signal quality?

21. Click the **Details** button. Notice the IPv4 address is the same address displayed as when you executed the `ipconfig` command.

22. Close the **Wireless Network Connection Status** dialog box buy clicking **Close**.

23. Notice the Wireless connection icon in the taskbar. Click the wireless connection icon. Then move the mouse pointer to **Adatum01**, but don't click on it.

| Question 20 | What is the Radio Type? |

24. Click **Adatum01** and then click **Disconnect**.

End of lab.

LAB 7
CONFIGURING STORAGE

THIS LAB CONTAINS THE FOLLOWING EXERCISES AND ACTIVITIES:

Exercise 7.1   Creating a Simple Volume

Exercise 7.2   Creating a Storage Pool and a Storage Space

Lab Challenge   Using Windows PowerShell to Configure Disks

BEFORE YOU BEGIN

The lab environment consists of student workstations connected to a local area network, along with a server that functions as the domain controller for a domain called adatum.com. The computers required for this lab are listed in Table 7-1.

Table 7-1
Computers required for Lab 7

Computer	Operating System	Computer Name
Server (VM 1)	Windows Server 2012 R2	LON-DC1
Client (VM 2)	Windows 10	LON-CL1

In addition to the computers, you will also require the software listed in Table 7-2 to complete Lab 7.

Table 7-2
Software required for Lab 7

Software	Location
Lab 7 student worksheet	Lab07_worksheet.docx (provided by instructor)

Working with Lab Worksheets

Each lab in this manual requires that you answer questions, shoot screen shots, and perform other activities that you will document in a worksheet named for the lab, such as Lab07_worksheet.docx. You will find these worksheets on the book companion site. It is recommended that you use a USB flash drive to store your worksheets, so you can submit them to your instructor for review. As you perform the exercises in each lab, open the appropriate worksheet file, fill in the required information, and then save the file to your flash drive.

SCENARIO

After completing this lab, you will be able to:

- Create a simple volume

- Create a storage pool and a storage space

- Use Windows PowerShell to manage disks

Estimated lab time: 40 minutes

Exercise 7.1	Creating a Simple Volume
Overview	In this exercise, you will first create a simple volume and then you will expand the simple volume.
Mindset	A simple volume is a type of volume that uses free space available on a single disk. Because it requires only a single disk, a simple volume is the quickest and easiest to set up.
Completion time	20 minutes

1. Log on to **LON-CL1** as **adatum\administrator** with the password of **Pa$$w0rd**.

2. On **LON-CL1**, right-click the **Start** button and choose **Disk Management**. Disk Management opens, as shown in Figure 7-1.

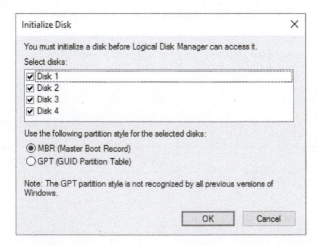

Figure 7-1
Managing Disks with Disk Management

Question 1	*Where else can you find Disk Management?*

3. When you are prompted to initialize disks, click **Cancel**.

4. Expand Disk Management to fill the entire screen.

5. Right-click the 10 GB disk (**Disk 4**) and choose **Initialize Disk**.

Question 2	*How many spare non-initialized disks do you have?*

6. In the Initialize Disk dialog box, click **OK**.

7. Right-click the 10 GB Unallocated disk and choose **New Simple Volume**.

8. In the New Simple Volume Wizard, on the Welcome screen, click **Next**.

9. On the Specify Volume Size page, for the Simple volume size in MB, type **5000** and then click **Next**.

10. On the Assign Drive Letter or Path screen, answer the following question. Then make sure that the assign the driver letter is **F** and click **Next**.

Question 3	*Which drive letter will be assigned to the new volume?*

11. On the Format Partition screen, answer the following question. Then in the Volume label text box, type **Data**. Click **Next**.

Question 4	*Which file system will the new volume use?*

12. On the Completing the New Simple Volume Wizard screen, click **Finish**.

13. If a message displays, stating that you need to format the disk, click the **Cancel** button. The message box is hidden behind Disk Management.

14. Take a screen shot of Disk Management showing the new volume by pressing **Alt+PrtScr** and then paste it into your Lab07_worksheet file in the page provided by pressing **Ctrl+V**.

15. To expand the new drive, right-click the partition that you just created (F drive) and choose **Extend Volume**.

16. In the Extend Volume Wizard, on the Welcome page, click **Next**.

17. On the Select Disks page, answer the following question and then click **Next**.

Question 5	*How much free disk space is available on Disk 2?*

18. On the Completing the Extend Volume Wizard page, click **Finish**.

19. Take a screen shot of Disk Management showing the new volume by pressing **Alt+PrtScr** and then paste it into your Lab07_worksheet file in the page provided by pressing **Ctrl+V**.

Remain logged on to LON-CL1 for the next exercise.

Exercise 7.2	Creating a Storage Pool and a Storage Space
Overview	In this exercise, you will create a storage pool and then you will create a storage space on a computer running Windows 10.
Mindset	To improve the performance and reliability of the disk system used in Windows 10, you can create storage pools and storage spaces to utilize disk space from multiple disks.
Completion time	10 minutes

1. On **LON-CL1**, right-click the **Start** button and choose **Control Panel**.

2. In the Control Panel pane, click **System and Security > Storage Spaces**.

3. On the Manage Storage Spaces page (see Figure 7-2), click **Create a new pool and storage space**.

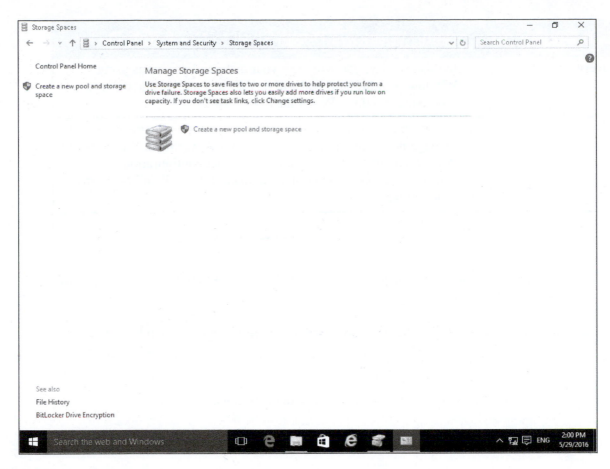

Figure 7-2
The Manage Storage Spaces page

4. On the Select drives to create a storage pool page, click **Create pool**.

Question 6	Which drive letter will be assigned to the Storage space?
Question 7	What is the default resiliency type?
Question 8	How many disk failures can a two-way mirror have before you lose the data?

5. Click the **Create storage space** button.

6. Take a screen shot showing the Manage Storage Spaces page by pressing **Alt+PrtScr** and then paste it into your Lab07_worksheet file in the page provided by pressing **Ctrl+V**.

End of exercise. Close any open windows before you begin the next exercise.

Lab Challenge	Using Windows PowerShell to Configure Disks
Overview	In this exercise, you will view your disks and partitions using Windows PowerShell. You will then format a drive and delete a disk using Windows PowerShell.
Mindset	Just as you can manage disks, volumes, and file systems with Disk Management, you can also use Windows PowerShell. Windows PowerShell allows for task automation and configuration management that consists of a command-line shell and associated scripting language.
Completion time	10 minutes

1. On **LON-CL1**, right-click the **Start** button and type **PowerShell**. From the search results, click **Windows PowerShell**.

2. From the Windows PowerShell window, execute the following command:

   ```
   Get-Disk
   ```

3. From the Windows PowerShell window, execute the following command:

   ```
   Get-Partition
   ```

Question 9	*How big is the C drive volume?*

4. To format the F drive, from the Windows PowerShell window, execute the following command:

   ```
   Format-volume -driveletter f
   ```

5. Take a screen shot showing the Windows PowerShell window by pressing **Alt+PrtScr** and then paste it into your Lab07_worksheet file in the page provided by pressing **Ctrl+V**.

6. Remove the partition/volumes by using the following command:

   ```
   Clear-disk 4 -RemoveData
   ```

7. When you are prompted to confirm that you want to erase all data on disk 4, type **y**.

End of lab.

LAB 8
CONFIGURING DATA ACCESS AND USAGE

THIS LAB CONTAINS THE FOLLOWING EXERCISES AND ACTIVITIES:

Exercise 8.1   Managing NTFS and Share Permissions

Exercise 8.2   Configuring Libraries

Exercise 8.3   Configuring Printers

Exercise 8.4   Supporting HomeGroups

Lab Challenge   Using OneDrive to Manage Files/Folders

BEFORE YOU BEGIN

The lab environment consists of student workstations connected to a local area network, along with a server that functions as the domain controller for a domain called adatum.com. The computers required for this lab are listed in Table 8-1.

Table 8-1
Computers required for Lab 8

Computer	Operating System	Computer Name
Server (VM 1)	Windows Server 2012 R2	LON-DC1
Client (VM 2)	Windows 10	LON-CL1
Client (VM 3)	Windows 10	LON-CL4

In addition to the computers, you will also require the software listed in Table 8-2 to complete Lab 8.

Table 8-2
Software required for Lab 8

Software	Location
Lab 8 student worksheet	Lab08_worksheet.docx (provided by instructor)

Working with Lab Worksheets

Each lab in this manual requires that you answer questions, shoot screen shots, and perform other activities that you will document in a worksheet named for the lab, such as Lab08_worksheet.docx. You will find these worksheets on the book companion site. It is recommended that you use a USB flash drive to store your worksheets, so you can submit them to your instructor for review. As you perform the exercises in each lab, open the appropriate worksheet file, fill in the required information, and then save the file to your flash drive.

SCENARIO

After completing this lab, you will be able to:

- Manage NTFS and share permissions

- Configure libraries

- Configure and manage printers

- Create and manage HomeGroups

- Use OneDrive to manage files/folders

Estimated lab time: 85 minutes

Exercise 8.1	Managing NTFS and Share Permissions
Overview	In this exercise, you will create a folder, share the folder, and then configure the NTFS and share permissions.
Mindset	As a Windows administrator, you need to know how to manage files and folders, including how to configure NTFS and share permissions so that users can access the files that they need in order to perform their jobs while preventing other users from accessing those same files.
Completion time	30 minutes

1. Log on to **LON-DC1** as **adatum\administrator** with the password of **Pa$$w0rd**.

2. On **LON-DC1**, using Server Manager, click **Tools > Active Directory Users and Computers**.

3. Right-click the **Users** OU and choose **New > User.**

4. In the New Object – User dialog box, type the following and then click **Next**.

    First Name: **Todd**

    Last Name: **Williams**

    User logon name: **TWilliams**

5. For the Password text box and the Confirm password text box, type **Pa$$w0rd**. Click to deselect **User must change password at next logon** and then select **Password never expires**. Click **Next**.

6. Click **Finish**.

7. Close **Active Directory Users and Computers**.

8. Log on to **LON-CL1** as **adatum\administrator** with the password of **Pa$$w0rd**.

9. On the taskbar, open File Explorer by clicking the **File Explorer** icon.

10. Under This PC, click **Local Disk (C:)**. Then right-click **Local Disk (C:)** and choose **New > Folder**. For the folder name, type **Data** and press **Enter**.

11. Right-click the **Data** folder and choose **Properties**.

12. Click the **Sharing** tab.

13. Click the **Advanced Sharing** button.

14. Click to select **Share this folder**.

15. To configure the share permissions, click the **Permissions** button.

16. With Everyone already selected, click to select **Allow Full Control**.

17. Click **OK** to close the Permission for Data dialog box.

18. Click **OK** to close the Advanced Sharing dialog box.

19. To manage the NTFS permissions, click the **Security** tab.

Question 1	*Which permissions do Authenticated Users have?*

20. Click the **Advanced** button.

21. In the Advanced Security Settings for Data dialog box (see Figure 8-1), click the **Effective Access** tab.

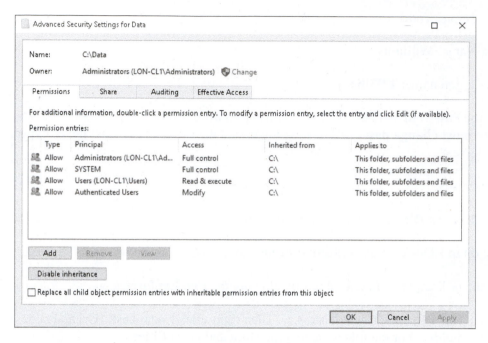

Figure 8-1
The Advanced Security Settings for Data dialog box

22. Click **Select a user**.

23. In the Select Users, Computers, Service Accounts, or Groups dialog box, in the Enter the object name to select text box, type **TWilliams** and then click **OK**.

24. Click the **View effective access** button.

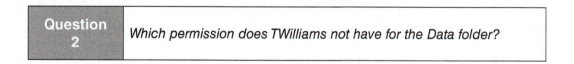

Question 2	Which permission does TWilliams not have for the Data folder?

25. Click **OK** to close the Advanced Security Settings for Data dialog box.

26. Click the **Edit** button.

27. In the Permissions for Data dialog box, click **Add**.

28. In the Select Users, Computers, Service Accounts, or Groups dialog box, in the Enter the object name to select text box, type **TWilliams** and then click **OK**.

29. With **TWilliams** selected, click to select **Allow Full control**.

30. Click **OK** to close the Permissions for Data dialog box.

31. In the Data Properties dialog box, click the **Advanced** button.

32. Click the **Effective Access** tab.

33. Click **Select a user**.

34. In the Select Users, Computers, Service Accounts, or Groups dialog box, in the Enter the object name to select text box, type **TWilliams** and then click **OK**.

35. Click the **View effective access** button.

Question 3	Which permission does TWilliams not *have for the Data folder?*

36. Take a screen shot of the Advanced Security Settings for Data dialog box by pressing **Alt+PrtScr** and then paste it into your Lab08_worksheet file in the page provided by pressing **Ctrl+V**.

37. Click **OK** to close the Advanced Security Settings for Data dialog box.

38. Click **Close** to close the Data Properties dialog box.

Close all windows on LON-CL1.

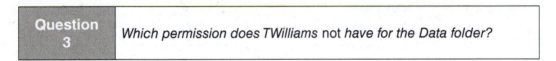

Exercise 8.2	Configuring Libraries
Overview	In this exercise, you will create a new library, which will combine multiple folders into the library.
Mindset	Although a library looks like an ordinary folder, it is a virtual folder that simply points to files and folders in different locations on a hard disk, network drive, or external drive.
Completion time	10 minutes

1. On LON-CL1, on the taskbar, open File Explorer by clicking the **File Explorer** icon.

2. If the libraries are not showing in the navigation pane, click the **View** tab and then click **Navigation pane > Show libraries**, as shown in Figure 8-2.

Figure 8-2
Selecting images to use

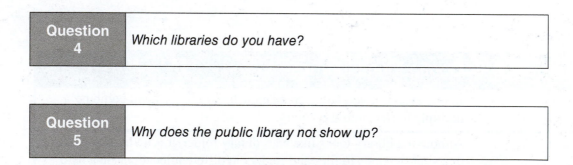

Question 4	Which libraries do you have?

Question 5	Why does the public library not show up?

3. Click the **Libraries** node and then expand the **Libraries** node.

4. In the navigation pane, click the **Libraries** node to select it. Then right-click **Libraries** and choose **New > Library**.

5. A Library node appears with the default name New Library. To rename the library, type **MyLibrary** and press **Enter**.

6. Click the **MyLibrary** library. Because the library was just created and is empty, click the **Include a folder** button.

7. In the Include Folder in MyLibrary dialog box, click the **Documents** folder and then click the **Include folder** button.

8. Right-click the **MyLibrary** library and choose **Properties**.

9. In the MyLibrary Properties dialog box, click the **Add** button.

10. In the Include Folder in MyLibrary dialog box, click the **Desktop** folder and then click **Include folder**.

11. Take a screen shot of the MyLibrary Properties dialog box window by pressing **Alt+PrtScr** and then paste it into your Lab08_worksheet file in the page provided by pressing **Ctrl+V**.

12. Close the MyLibrary Properties dialog box by clicking **OK**.

Exercise 8.3	Configuring Printers
Overview	In this exercise, you will first install a local printer on one system. You will then configure a printer and include permissions. Finally, you will install a printer on another system that points to the shared printer on the first system.
Mindset	With network printing, multiple users can share the same printer. This is a cost-effective solution when you administer several employees who are located in different locations.
Completion time	20 minutes

1. Log on to **LON-CL1** as **adatum\administrator** with the password of **Pa$$w0rd**.

2. On **LON-CL1**, right-click the **Start** button and choose **Control Panel**.

3. Under Hardware and Sound, click **View devices and printers**. The Devices and Printers page opens (see Figure 8-3).

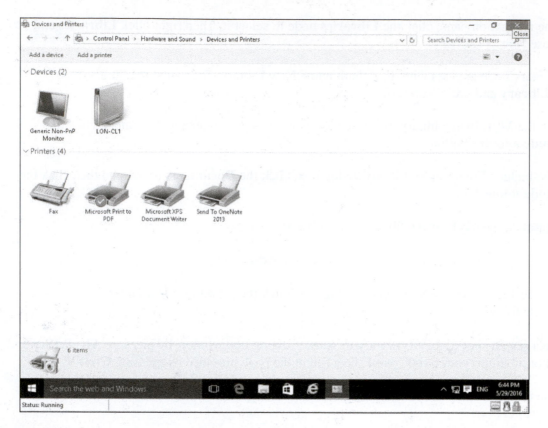

Figure 8-3
The Devices and Printers page

4. At the top of the page, click **Add a Printer**.

5. If there was a printer connected to a USB port, Windows would most likely find the printer. However, since a printer is not connected, wait until the search has completed and then click **The printer that I want isn't listed**.

6. In the Add Printer wizard, select **Add a local printer or network printer with manual settings** and then click **Next**.

7. On the Choose a printer port page, answer the following question and then click **Next**.

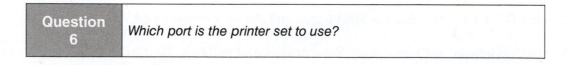

| Question 6 | Which port is the printer set to use? |

8. On the Install the printer driver page, for the Manufacturer, click **HP**. Then for the Printers, click **HP Color LaserJet 1600 Class Driver**. Click **Next**.

9. On the Type a Printer Name page, click **Next**.

10. On the Printer Sharing page, change the share name to **HPColorLJ1600**, and then click **Next**.

11. Click the **Finish** button.

12. Take a screen shot of the Devices and Printers page by pressing **Alt+PrtScr** and then paste it into your Lab08_worksheet file in the page provided by pressing **Ctrl+V**.

13. Right-click the **HP Color LaserJet 1600 Class Driver** printer and choose **Printer Properties**.

14. In the HP Color LaserJet 1600 Class Driver Properties dialog box, click the **Sharing** tab. Notice the *Share* name.

15. For the printer to be listed in Active Directory, click to select **List in the directory**.

16. Click the **Ports** tab. Notice the port that is assigned.

17. Click the **Security** tab.

Question 7	Who is allowed to print to this printer?

18. Click the **Administrators** group.

Question 8	Which permissions are assigned to Administrators?

19. Click **Everyone**.

20. Select the **Allow Manage documents** permission.

21. Close the HP Color LaserJet 1600 Class Driver Properties dialog box by clicking **OK**.

22. Log on to **LON-CL4** as **adatum\administrator** with the password of **Pa$$w0rd**.

23. On **LON-CL4**, click the **Start** button. Type **\\LON-CL1** and press **Enter**.

24. Right-click the **HPColorLJ1600** printer and choose **Connect**.

25. Click the **Start** button and then click **Settings**.

26. On the Settings page, click **Devices**.

27. Take a screen shot of the Devices page by pressing **Alt+PrtScr** and then paste it into your Lab08_worksheet file in the page provided by pressing **Ctrl+V**.

Exercise 8.4	Supporting HomeGroups
Overview	In this exercise, you will create a HomeGroup on a computer running Windows 10.
Mindset	A HomeGroup is a group of computers on a home network that can share files and printers. To protect your HomeGroup, you can use a password. Similar to share permissions, other users cannot change the files that you share unless you give them permission to do so.
Completion time	15 minutes

1. On **LON-CL4**, right-click the **Start** button and choose **Control Panel**.

2. In the Control Panel, click **Network and Internet > Network and Sharing Center**.

3. On the Network and Sharing Center page, click the **HomeGroup** link at the bottom of the screen. The HomeGroup page opens (as shown in Figure 8-4).

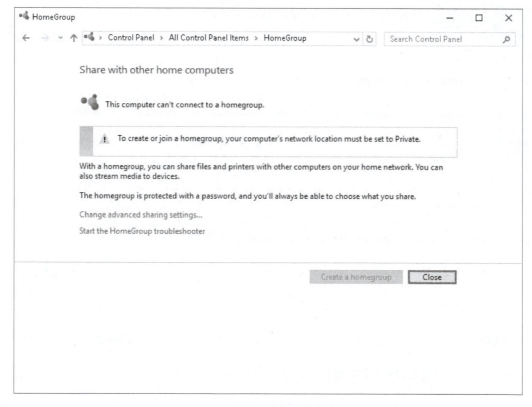

Figure 8-4
Managing HomeGroups

Question 9	*Why is the Create a homegroup button greyed out?*

4. Click the **Start the HomeGroup troubleshooter**.

5. When the troubshooter opens, click **Next**.

6. When you are prompted to troubleshoot network problems, click **Skip this step**.

7. When you are prompted to change the network location to Private, click **Apply this fix**.

8. When the problem is fixed, click **Close**.

9. Click **Create a homegroup** button.

10. In the Create a HomeGroup wizard, click **Next**.

Question 10	By default, which library or folder is shared

11. Click **Next**.

Question 11	What is the password to add other computers to your homegroup?

12. Click **Finish**.

13. Take a screen shot of the HomeGroup page by pressing **Alt+PrtScr** and then paste the resulting image into the Lab08_worksheet file in the page provided by pressing **Ctrl+V**.

Log off LON-CL4.

Lab Challenge	Using OneDrive to Manage Files/Folders
Overview	In this exercise, you will use OneDrive online to create a folder and a document. You will then download the document to your desktop and delete the document. Finally, you will upload a document from your desktop.
Mindset	OneDrive is a file hosting service that allows you to store and create files and folders and share them with other users and groups. OneDrive for Business is different from the public version of OneDrive because OneDrive for Business is based on SharePoint. By using SharePoint, OneDrive for Business can be used by team members to store and work on documents with others and it helps ensure that business files for your users are stored in a central location.
Completion time	10 minutes

NOTE	*You will not be able to perform this exercise on the MOAC Labs Online systems. Instead, you need to use a computer running Windows 10 with access to the Internet. If your classroom has a dedicated Windows Server 2012 R2 or Windows Server 2016, you can use a virtual machine running Windows 10.*

1. Log on to a Windows 10 computer that is connected to the Internet.

2. Open **Internet Explorer** and go to **http://onedrive.live.com**. If you are not automatically logged on, click **Sign In** and sign in with your Office 365 credentials. When you are logged on, you should see a Welcome to OneDrive page similar to what is shown in Figure 8-5.

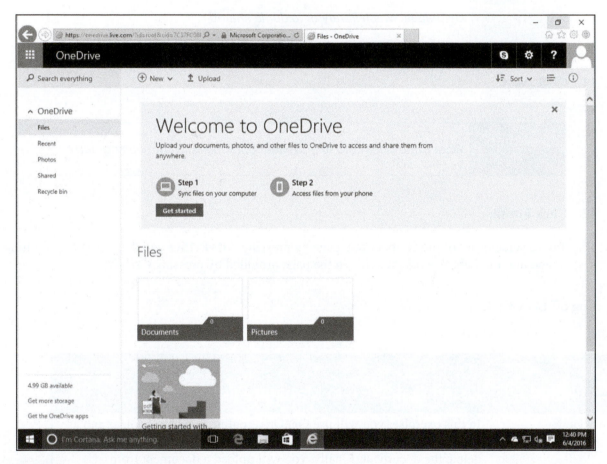

Figure 8-5
Using OneDrive

3. Click the **Documents** folder.

4. From the menu at the top of the page, click **New > Folder**.

5. In the Folder text box, type **Project Files** and then click the **Create** button.

6. Click the **Project Files** folder.

7. From the menu at the top of the page, click **New > Word document**.

8. Type a few words in the document. As you type text, the Word document will be saved frequently.

9. To specify a file name, click Document at the top of the window and then replace that name by typing **Project Scope**.

10. Click the **Project Files** link (located at the upper-left corner, next to Word Online) to return to the main screen.

11. Take a screen shot of the OneDrive page by pressing **Alt+PrtScr** and then paste it into your Lab08_worksheet file in the page provided by pressing **Ctrl+V**.

12. Right-click the **Project Scope** document and choose **Download**.

13. When you are prompted to open or save Project Scope.docx, click the down arrow next to save and then click **Save as**.

14. Select the **Desktop** folder (if it is not already selected) and then click the **Save** button.

15. To delete the Project Scope document, right-click the **Project Scope** document and choose **Delete**.

16. Take a screen shot of the OneDrive page by pressing **Alt+PrtScr** and then paste it into your Lab08_worksheet file in the page provided by pressing **Ctrl+V**.

17. Shrink the Internet Explorer window so that it displays only on half the desktop and so that you can see the Project Scope document that you saved on the desktop.

18. Drag the **Project Scope.docx** document to the "This folder is empty" space.

19. Close **Internet Explorer**.

End of lab.

LAB 9
IMPLEMENTING APPS

THIS LAB CONTAINS THE FOLLOWING EXERCISES AND ACTIVITIES:

Exercise 9.1   Signing Up for Microsoft Intune

Exercise 9.2   Sideloading a Windows Store App to Microsoft Intune

Exercise 9.3   Managing Default Apps

Exercise 9.4   Managing Desktop Applications

Lab Challenge   Managing Windows Store Apps

BEFORE YOU BEGIN

The lab environment consists of student workstations connected to a local area network, along with a server that functions as the domain controller for a domain called adatum.com. The computers required for this lab are listed in Table 9-1.

Table 9-1
Computers required for Lab 9

Computer	Operating System	Computer Name
Server (VM 1)	Windows Server 2012 R2	LON-DC1
Server (VM 2)	Windows 10	LON-CL1
Client (VM 3)	Windows 10	Computer with Internet access

In addition to the computers, you will also require the software listed in Table 9-2 to complete Lab 9.

Table 9-2
Software required for Lab 9

Software	Location
Microsoft PowerPoint Viewer (PowerPointViewer.exe)	\\Lon-dc1\Software
Lab 9 student worksheet	Lab09_worksheet.docx (provided by instructor)

Working with Lab Worksheets

Each lab in this manual requires that you answer questions, shoot screen shots, and perform other activities that you will document in a worksheet named for the lab, such as Lab09_worksheet.docx. You will find these worksheets on the book companion site. It is recommended that you use a USB flash drive to store your worksheets, so you can submit them to your instructor for review. As you perform the exercises in each lab, open the appropriate worksheet file, fill in the required information, and then save the file to your flash drive.

SCENARIO

After completing this lab, you will be able to:

■ Sign up for Microsoft Intune

■ Sideload a Windows Store app to Microsoft Intune

■ Manage default apps

■ Manage desktop applications

■ Manage Windows Store apps

Estimated lab time: 85 minutes

Exercise 9.1	Signing Up for Microsoft Intune
Overview	In this exercise, you will sign up for a Microsoft Intune account.
Mindset	Microsoft Intune is a cloud-based management solution that allows you to manage your computers and mobile devices when they are connected to or not connected to the corporate network. Microsoft Intune helps you manage your computers and mobile devices through a web console.
Completion time	20 minutes

> | NOTE | *You will not be able to perform this exercise on the MOAC Labs Online systems. Instead, you need to use a computer running Windows 10 with access to the Internet. If your classroom has a dedicated Windows Server 2012 R2 or Windows Server 2016, you can use a virtual machine running Windows 10.* |
> | --- | --- |

1. On the computer running Windows 10 that is connected to the Internet, open **Internet Explorer**.

2. Go to **http://www.microsoft.com/en-us/server-cloud/products/microsoft-intune/** and click **Try Now**.

3. On the signup page (as shown in Figure 9-1), type the following information and then click **Next**:

   Country or Region: **<Your country or region>**

   First name: **<Your first name>**

   Last name: **<Your last name>**

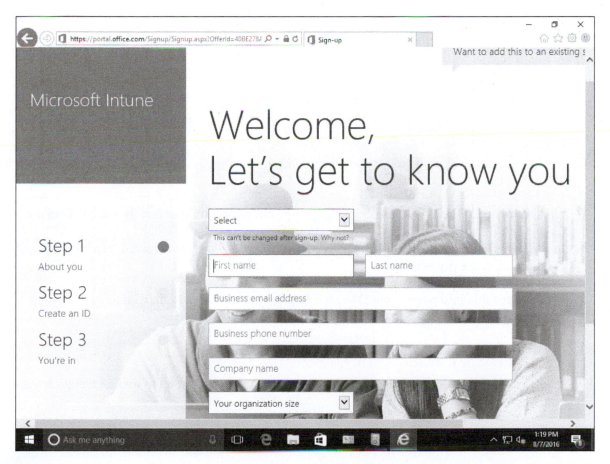

Figure 9-1
Creating a Microsoft Intune account

Business email address: **<Your email address>**

Business phone number: **<Your phone number>**

Company name: **<Your last name> Corporation**

Your organization size: **25-49 people**

4. On the Create your user ID page, type the following information.

    User name: **<FirstInitial><LastName>**

    Therefore, if your name is John Smith, you would type the following:

    JSmith

5. For your company, type:

    <FirstName><LastName>Training<Month><Year>

    Therefore, if your name is John Smith and you are performing this lab in February 2017, you would type the following:

    JohnSmithTraining022017 (in front of .onmicrosoft.com)

Question 1	*Record your company name.*

6. For the Create new password text box and the Confirm new password text box, type **Pa$$w0rd**. Click **Next**.

7. On the Prove. You're. Not. A. Robot. page, type your phone number and then click **Text me**.

8. In the Enter your verification code text box, type the code that you received on your phone and then click **Create my account**.

9. On the Save this info page, record the sign-in page and user ID and then click **You're ready to go**.

10. On the Get Started with Microsoft Intune page, click **Start**.

11. In the Office 365 Admin center, click the Admin centers icon (last icon) and then click **Intune** (see Figure 9-2). Log in to Intune.

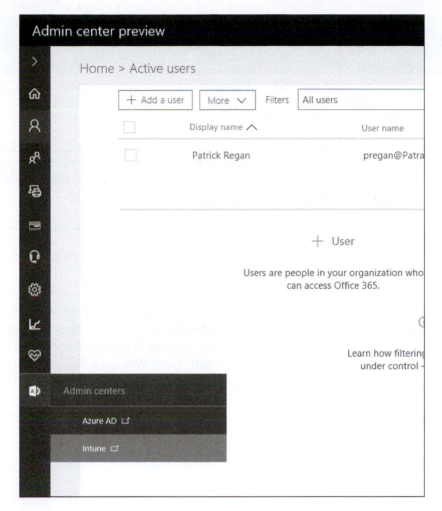

Figure 9-2
Creating a Microsoft Intune account

12. If a message appears, indicating the application requires Microsoft Silverlight, click **Get Microsoft Silverlight**. When you are prompted to run or save Silverlight_x64.exe, click **Run**. If the User Account Control dialog box displays, click **Yes**.

13. In the Install Silverlight dialog box, click **Install now**. When you are prompted to enable Microsoft Update, click **Next**. Click **Close**.

14. If you are prompted to log in, type **Pa$$w0rd** in the Password text box.

15. Click the **Admin** icon.

16. Take a screen shot of the Administration Overview page by pressing **Alt+PrtScr** and then paste it into your Lab09_worksheet file in the page provided by pressing **Ctrl+V**.

17. Close **Internet Explorer**.

Exercise 9.2	Sideloading a Windows Store App to Microsoft Intune
Overview	In this exercise, you will download the PowerPoint Viewer and upload the executable to Microsoft Intune and then configure Microsoft Intune so that it can be deployed to your Microsoft Intune clients.
Mindset	There are several ways in which you can install applications using Microsoft Intune. One method is Sideloading, which is the process of installing Windows Store applications without using the Windows Store.
Completion time	20 minutes

NOTE	*You will not be able to perform this exercise on the MOAC Labs Online systems. Instead, you need to use a computer running Windows 10 with access to the Internet. If your classroom has a dedicated Windows Server 2012 R2 or Windows Server 2016, you can use a virtual machine running Windows 10.*

1. Click the **File Explorer** icon on the taskbar.

2. Navigate to the **C:** folder.

3. At the top of the window, click the **New folder** button. For the folder name, type **Software**.

4. On the computer running Windows 10 that is connected to the Internet, open **Internet Explorer**.

5. Go to **https://www.microsoft.com/en-us/download/details.aspx?id=13** and download **PowerPoint Viewer**. Save the PowerPoint Viewer to the **C:\Software** folder.

6. Go to the Microsoft Intune website (**https://manage.microsoft.com**) and log in to Microsoft Intune.

7. Click the **Apps** workspace, as shown in Figure 9-3.

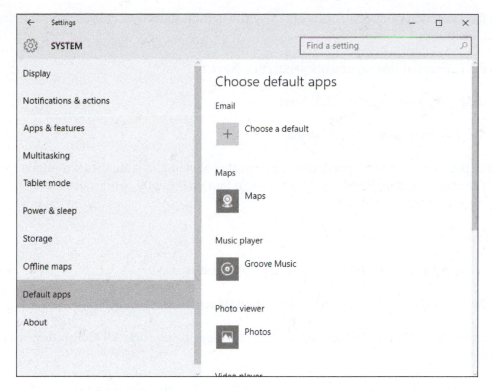

Figure 9-3
Accessing the Apps workspace

8. Under Tasks, click **Add Apps**. If you are prompted to confirm that you want to run Microsoft Intune Software Publisher, click **Run**. If you are asked to sign in, log in with an administrator account for Intune.

9. In the Add Software Wizard, on the Before you begin page, click **Next**. The Software Setup page opens.

Question 2	What are the default software installer file types?

10. In the Specify the location of the software setup files text box, click **C:\Software\ PowerPointViewer.exe** and then click **Next**.

11. On the Software description page, in the Publisher text box, type **Microsoft**. Click **Next**.

12. On the Requirements page, answer the following question and then click **Next**.

Question 3	What is the default architecture and the default operating system?

13. On the Detection rules page, select the **Use the default detection rules** option and then click **Next**.

14. On the Command line arguments page, click **Next**.

15. On the Returns codes page, click **Next**.

16. On the Summary page, click **Upload**.

17. When the software is uploaded, take a screen shot showing that the data was uploaded success-fully by pressing **Alt+PrtScr** and then paste it into your Lab09_worksheet file in the page provided by pressing **Ctrl+V**.

18. Click **Close**.

19. Click the **Apps** workspace and then click **Apps Status**.

20. At the top of the window, click **Manage Deployment**.

21. In the Deploy Software Wizard, on the Select Groups page, click **All Computers** and then click **Add**. Click **Next**.

22. On the Deployment Action page, under Approval, select **Required Install** from the pull-down menu. For the Deadline, select **One month**.

23. Click **Finish**.

24. Take a screen shot showing your Apps, including the Deployed column, by pressing **Alt+PrtScr** and then paste it into your Lab09_worksheet file in the page provided by pressing **Ctrl+V**. You may need to adjust the columns to show the Deployed colum.

25. Close **Internet Explorer**.

Exercise 9.3	Managing Default Apps
Overview	In this exercise, you will configure the default apps and programs associated with a data file.
Mindset	Because those applications are running in the Windows 10 desktop environment, there are centralized settings that you can configure each application, including specifying which files are associated with an application.
Completion time	10 minutes

1. Log on to **LON-CL1** as **adatum\administrator** with the password of **Pa$$w0rd**.

2. On **LON-CL1**, click the **Start** button and then click **Settings**.

3. On the Settings page, click **System**.

4. On the System page, click the **Default apps** vertical tab.

Question 4	*What is the default program for the Photo viewer?*

5. To change the primary web browser from Microsoft Edge to Microsoft Internet Explorer, scroll down to Web browser, click **Microsoft Edge**, and then select **Internet Explorer**.

6. Take a screen shot showing the Web browser by pressing **Alt+PrtScr** and then paste it into your Lab09_worksheet file in the page provided by pressing **Ctrl+V**.

7. To reset the Microsoft recommended default apps, click the **Reset** button. When the applications have been reset, a checkmark will appear next to the Reset button.

8. Click the **Choose default apps by file type** option.

9. On the Choose default apps by file type page, scroll down to .gif.

Question 5	*What is the default program to open .gif files?*

10. To change the default program for .gif files, click **Photo** and then select **Paint**.

11. Close the **Settings** page.

Leave LON-CL1 open for the next exercise.

Exercise 9.4	Managing Desktop Applications
Overview	In this exercise, you will manage desktop applications, including installing and uninstalling desktop applications and configuring compatibility settings.
Mindset	To manage installed desktop programs, use the Programs and Features page. To overcome compatibility issues, you can manually configure the compatibility settings for an executable file. To access these settings, right-click the executable file, choose Properties, and then click the Compatibility tab.
Completion time	20 minutes

1. On **LON-CL1**, on the taskbar, click the **File Explorer** tile.

2. Using File Explorer, open the **\\LON-DC1\Software** folder.

3. Double-click the **PowerPointViewer.exe** program.

4. When the Microsoft Software License Terms are displayed, select the **Click here to accept the Microsoft Software License Terms** option and then click **Continue**.

5. In the Microsoft PowerPoint Viewer Setup wizard, on the Welcome page, click **Next**.

Question 6	What is the default installation location for the PowerPoint Viewer program?

6. Click the **Install** button.

7. When the program is installed, click **OK**.

8. Using File Explorer, open the **C:\Program Files (x86)\Microsoft Office** folder.

9. Double-click the **Office14 f**older.

10. Right-click the **PPTVIEW.EXE** program and choose **Properties**.

11. In the PPTVIEW.EXE Properties dialog box, click the **Compatibility** tab (see Figure 9-4.

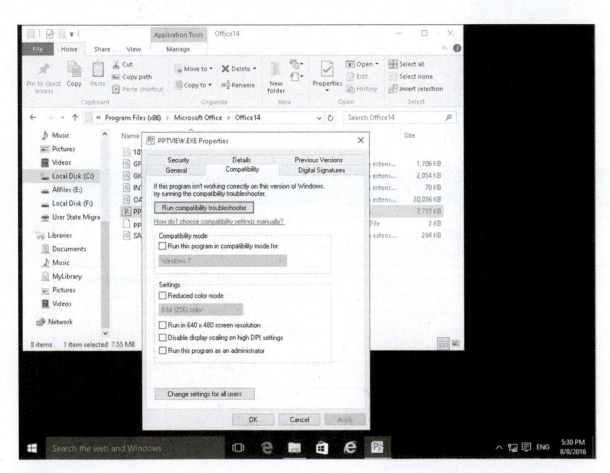

Figure 9-4
Managing program compatibility settings

12. To run this program in Windows 7 compatibility mode, select the **Run this program in compatibility mode for** option.

13. To allow this program to run as an administrator, select the **Run this program as an administrator** option.

14. Take a screen shot showing that compatibility settings by pressing **Alt+PrtScr** and then paste it into your Lab09_worksheet file in the page provided by pressing **Ctrl+V**.

15. Close the PPTVIEW.EXE Properties dialog box by clicking **OK**.

16. Right-click the **Start** button and choose **Programs and Features**.

17. On the Control Panel Programs and Features page, click the **Microsoft PowerPoint Viewer** program.

Question 7	What are the two options that you can perform with the Microsoft PowerPoint Viewer program?

18. Click the **Uninstall** option.

19. When you are prompted to confirm that you want to uninstall Microsoft PowerPoint Viewer, click **Yes**.

20. Take a screen shot showing the Programs and Features page by pressing **Alt+PrtScr** and then paste it into your Lab09_worksheet file in the page provided by pressing **Ctrl+V**.

21. Close the Programs and Features page.

Log off LON-CL1.

Lab Challenge	Managing Windows Store Apps
Overview	In this exercise, you will manage your Windows Store settings. You will then find and install PowerPoint Mobile.
Mindset	The Windows Store provides a central location for you to purchase and download Windows apps that run on Windows 8 and later operating systems. Windows store apps are special types of apps that work on computers that are running Windows 8 and newer. Windows Store apps do not run on Windows 7 or earlier versions of Windows and they tend to be smaller and faster than desktop apps.
Completion time	15 minutes

NOTE	*You will not be able to perform this exercise on the MOAC Labs Online systems. Instead, you need to use a computer running Windows 10 with access to the Internet. If your classroom has a dedicated Windows Server 2012 R2 or Windows Server 2016, you can use a virtual machine running Windows 10.*

1. Log on to a computer running Windows 10 that has access to the Internet.

2. On the taskbar, click the **Windows Store** button.

3. Sign in to the Windows Store by clicking the **Sign In** button and then clicking **Sign In**. Then log in with your Microsoft account credentials.

4. Click the user icon and then click **Settings**. The Settings page opens, as shown in Figure 9-5.

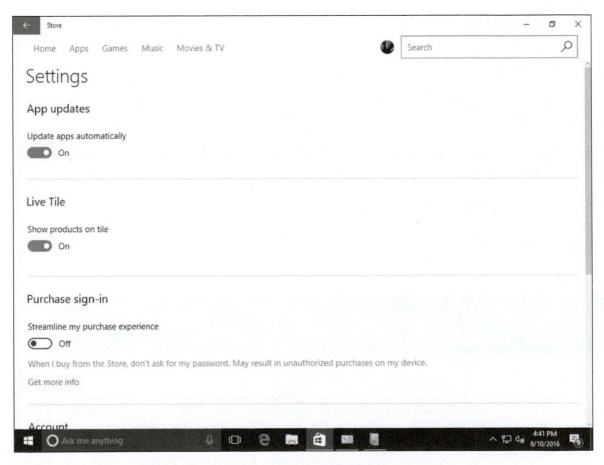

Figure 9-5
Managing Windows Store settings

5. To update apps automatically, ensure that the **Update apps automatically options is set to On**. If it is not, just click the **Update apps automatically** option.

6. To streamline your purchases so that you will not be asked for a password, ensure the **Streamline my purchase experience** is set to **On**. If it is not, just click the **Streamline my purchase experience** option.

7. At the top of the window, click the **Apps** option. Then, in the search text box, type **PowerPoint** and click the **Search** button. From the search results, click **PowerPoint Mobile**.

8. When the product is installed, take a screen shot by pressing **Alt+PrtScr** and then paste it into your Lab09_worksheet file in the page provided by pressing **Ctrl+V**.

9. To view your Downloads and updates, click the user icon again and then click **Downloads and updates**.

Question 8	Which apps do you already have?

10. At the top of the window, click the **Check for updates** button.

11. Click the user icon and then click the **Downloads and updates** option.

12. Take a screen shot that shows that the Microsoft Store has been updated recently by pressing **Alt+PrtScr** and then paste it into your Lab09_worksheet file in the page provided by pressing **Ctrl+V**.

13. Close the Windows Store.

14. Click the **Start** button, find and right-click the **PowerPoint Mobile** program, click **Uninstall**, and then click the **Uninstall** button.

15. When PowerPoint Mobile is uninstalled, take a screen shot showing the all apps page by pressing **Alt+PrtScr** and then paste it into your Lab09_worksheet file in the page provided by pressing **Ctrl+V**.

16. Close all windows.

End of lab.

LAB 10
CONFIGURING REMOTE MANAGEMENT

THIS LAB CONTAINS THE FOLLOWING EXERCISES AND ACTIVITIES:

Exercise 10.1   Configuring Remote Desktop

Exercise 10.2   Configuring Remote Assistance

Exercise 10.3   Manage a Remote System using the Microsoft Management Console

Lab Challenge   Running PowerShell Commands on a Remote Computer

BEFORE YOU BEGIN

The lab environment consists of student workstations connected to a local area network, along with a server that functions as the domain controller for a domain called adatum.com. The computers required for this lab are listed in Table 10-1.

Table 10-1
Computers required for Lab 10

Computer	Operating System	Computer Name
Server (VM 1)	Windows Server 2012 R2	LON-DC1
Server (VM 2)	Windows 10	LON-CL1
Client (VM 3)	Windows 10	LON-CL2

In addition to the computers, you will also require the software listed in Table 10-2 to complete Lab 10.

Table 10-2
Software required for Lab 10

Software	Location
Lab 10 student worksheet	Lab10_worksheet.docx (provided by instructor)

Working with Lab Worksheets

Each lab in this manual requires that you answer questions, shoot screen shots, and perform other activities that you will document in a worksheet named for the lab, such as Lab10_worksheet.docx. You will find these worksheets on the book companion site. It is recommended that you use a USB flash drive to store your worksheets, so you can submit them to your instructor for review. As you perform the exercises in each lab, open the appropriate worksheet file, fill in the required information, and then save the file to your flash drive.

SCENARIO

After completing this lab, you will be able to:

- ◼ Configure Remote Desktop

- ◼ Configure Remote Assistance

- ◼ Manage a system remotely with the Microsoft Management Console

- ◼ Run Windows PowerShell commands on a remote computer

Estimated lab time: 70 minutes

Exercise 10.1	Configuring Remote Desktop
Overview	In this exercise, you will check the settings that allow a remote desktop connection. You will then use the Remote Desktop Connection (RDC) program to access a server using various settings.
Mindset	The Remote Desktop Protocol (RDP) is a proprietary protocol that was developed by Microsoft to connect to another computer over a network connection using the same graphical interface that you would use if you were sitting in front of the physical server. Typically, this would be done with Remote Desktop Connection (RDC), which would allow you to connect to a Remote Desktop Session Host or to a Remote Application.
Completion time	20 minutes

1. Log on to **LON-CL1** as **adatum\administrator** with the password of **Pa$$w0rd**.

2. On **LON-CL1**, right-click the **Start** button and choose **System**.

3. In the System window, click **Remote settings**. The System Properties dialog box opens with the Remote tab selected, as shown in Figure 10-1.

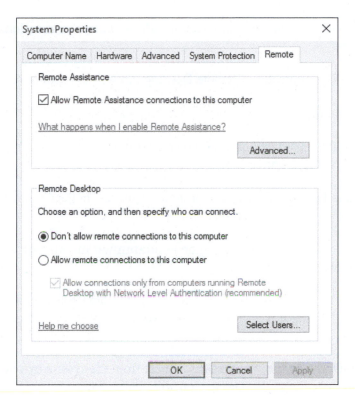

Figure 10-1
Managing Remote settings

Question 1	Does LON-CL1 allow users to connect to the system remotely using RDP?

4. Select the **Allow remote connections to this computer** option.

5. Click the **Select Users** button. The Remote Desktop Users dialog box opens.

Question 2	Which users can connect to this computer using RDP?

6. Close the Remote Desktop Users dialog box by clicking the **OK** button.

7. Close System Properties dialog box by clicking the **OK** button.

8. Close the System window.

9. Log on to LON-DC1 as **adatum\administrator** with the password of **Pa$$w0rd**.

10. Right-click the **Start** button and choose **System**.

11. In the System window, click **Remote settings**.

12. In the System Properties dialog box, select the **Allow remote connections to this computer** option.

13. When you a message indicates a Remote Desktop Firewall exception will be enabled, click **OK**.

14. Close the System Properties dialog box by clicking **OK**.

15. On LON-CL1, click the **Start** button and then type **remote desktop**. From the search results, click **Remote Desktop Connection**.

16. When the Remote Desktop Connection program launches, in the Computer text box, type **LON-DC1** and then click the **Connect** button.

17. In the Windows Security dialog box, log on as **adatum\administrator** with the password of **Pa$$w0rd** and then click **OK**.

18. Take a screen shot of the Settings page showing the remote desktop connection by pressing **Alt+PrtScr** and then paste it into your Lab10_worksheet file in the page provided by pressing **Ctrl+V**.

19. Close the LON-DC1 window and then disconnect from the system by clicking the **x** at the top of the window and then click **OK**. The session will continue to run.

20. Click the **Start** button and then type **remote desktop**. From the search results, click **Remote Desktop Connection**.

21. Click the **Show Options** button.

22. When the dialog box expands, click the **Display** tab.

Question 3	*What is the display configuration set to?*

23. Change the display configuration to **800 by 600 pixels** by sliding the slide bar to the left.

24. Click the **Local Resources** tab.

25. Click the **More** button.

26. In the Local devices and resources dialog box, expand the **Drives** node, select the **Local Disk (C:)**, and then click the **OK** button.

27. Click the **Connect** button. When you are prompted to confirm that you trust the remote connection, click **Connect**.

28. In the Windows Security dialog box, log on as **adatum\administrator** with the password of **Pa$$w0rd** and then click **OK**.

29. Take a screen shot of the Settings page showing the remote desktop connection by pressing **Alt+PrtScr** and then paste it into your Lab10_worksheet file in the page provided by pressing **Ctrl+V**.

30. In the LON-DC1 Remote Desktop Connection window, open File Explorer by clicking **File Explorer** on the taskbar.

Question 4	How does the Lon-CL1 C drive show up as?

31. Double-click **C on LON-CL1**. You are now browsing files on your LON-CL1.

32. Log off LON-DC1.

Question 5	During a Remote Desktop session, explain the result of opening the Network Connections window on the remote computer and configuring the network adapter to use a different IP address.

Leave LON-CL1 open for the next exercise.

Exercise 10.2	Configuring Remote Assistance
Overview	In this exercise, you will establish a Remote Assistance invitation on LON-CL2 and then use LON-CL1 to connect to LON-CL2 to perform some remote actions.
Mindset	Remote Assistance is a Windows 10 feature that enables an administrator, trainer, or support person to connect to a remote user's computer, chat with the user, and either view all of the user's activities or take complete control of the system. Similar to Remote Desktop, it also uses TCP port 3389.
Completion time	20 minutes

1. Log on to **LON-CL2**, as **adatum\administrator** with the password of **Pa$$w0rd**.

2. Right-click the **Start** button and choose **Control Panel**.

3. In the Control Panel, click **System and Security**. In the System section, click **Launch remote assistance**.

4. In the Windows Remote Assistance dialog box (see Figure 10-2), click **Invite someone you trust to help you**.

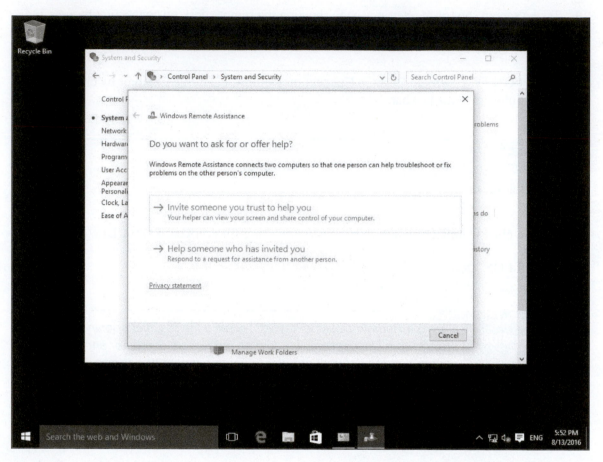

Figure 10-2
Asking for help with Windows Remote Assistance

5. On the How do you want to invite your trusted helper? page, click **Save this invitation as a file**.

6. In the Save As dialog box, in the File name text box, type **\\LON-DC1\Software\Invitation** and then click the **Save** button.

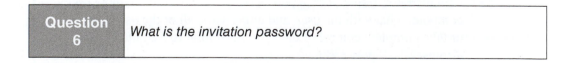

Question 6	What is the invitation password?

7. On LON-CL1, in the Control Panel, click **System and Security**. In the System section, click **Launch remote assistance.**

8. On the Do you want to ask for or offer help? page, click the **Help someone who has invited you** option.

9. On the Choose a way to connect to the other person's computer page, click **Use an invitation file**.

10. When the open dialog box opens, in the File Name text box, type **\\LON-DC1\Software\ Invitation** and then click the **Open** button.

11. When you are prompted to enter the password to connect to the remote computer, type the password that you recorded in Question 6, and then click **OK**.

12. On **LON-CL2**, when you are prompted to allow administrator to connect to your computer, click **Yes**.

13. On **LON-CL1**, take a screen shot of the Windows Remote Assistance window by pressing **Alt+PrtScr** and then paste it into your Lab10_worksheet file in the page provided by pressing **Ctrl+V**.

14. On **LON-CL1**, click the **Request control** button located at the top of the screen.

15. On **LON-CL2**, when you are prompted to confirm that you would like to allow an administrator to share control of the desktop, click **Yes**.

16. On **LON-CL1**, close the Control Panel on LON-CL2.

17. On **LON-CL1**, click the **Chat** button. Then in the chat text box, type **Hello** and click **Send**.

18. On **LON-CL2**, in the chat window, type **Thanks for your help** and then click **Send**.

19. On **LON-CL1**, take a screen shot of the Settings page showing the Windows Remote Assistance window by pressing **Alt+PrtScr** and then paste it into your Lab10_worksheet file in the page provided by pressing **Ctrl+V**.

20. On LON-CL1, click the **Stop sharing** button.

Close any open windows on LON-CL1 and LON-CL2.

Exercise 10.3	Managing a Remote System using the Microsoft Management Console
Overview	In this exercise, you will create a custom Microsoft Management Console (MMC) using the Computer Management snap-in. You will then use the Computer Management snap-in to manage a remote computer.
Mindset	When assisting users with computer problems or maintaining systems, you often need to check computer events, look at computer resource usage, or examine a disk's partition, among other tasks. You can use MMC tools and utilities for this purpose.
Completion time	15 minutes

1. On **LON-CL1**, right-click the **Start** button, type **mmc** in the Run box, and then press **Enter**.

2. In the MMC Console window, click **File > Add/Remove Snap-in**. The Add or Remove Snap-ins dialog box displays (see in Figure 10-3).

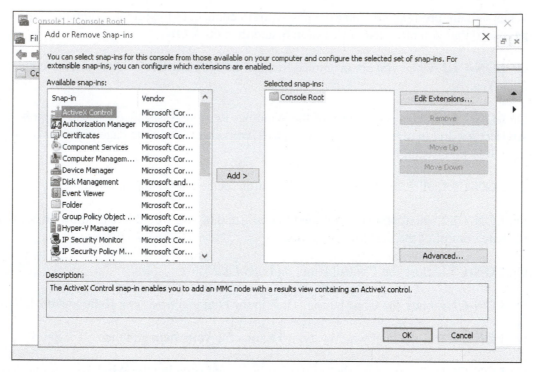

Figure 10-3
Adding an MMC snap-in

3. In the Available snap-ins list on the left, click **Computer Management**, and in the middle of the dialog box, click the **Add** button.

4. In the Computer Management dialog box, Local computer is already selected. Click **Finish**.

Question 7	To manage local user certificates and local computer certificates, how many snap-ins would you have to add to MMC?

5. Close the Add or Remove Snap-ins dialog box by clicking **OK**.

6. Expand the **Computer Management** node.

7. Right-click the Computer Management (Local) node and choose **Connect to another computer**.

8. In the Select Computer dialog box, select the **Another computer**. Then in the Another computer text box, type **LON-CL2**, and click **OK**.

9. When you receive a Computer Management message indicating that the computer cannot be managed, either the computer is not available, or a firewall is blocking the necessary traffic, close the message by clicking **OK**.

10. On **LON-CL2**, right-click the **Start** button and choose **Control Panel**.

11. In the Control Panel, click **System and Security > Windows Firewall**.

12. Click the **Turn Windows Firewall on or off** option.

13. For the domain network settings, select the **Turn off Windows Firewall** option and then click **OK**.

14. Go back to LON-CL1 and then right-click the Computer Management (Local) node and choose **Connect to another computer**.

15. In the Select Computer dialog box, select the **Another computer**. Then in the Another computer text box, type **LON-CL2** and click **OK**.

16. Expand the Event Viewer node, expand the **Windows Logs** node, and then click the **System** node.

17. On **LON-CL1**, take a screen shot showing the Windows Remote Assistance page by pressing **Alt+PrtScr** and then paste it into your Lab10_worksheet file in the page provided by pressing **Ctrl+V**.

18. In the MMC console, expand the **Services and Applications** node and then click **Services**.

19. Right-click the **Computer Browser** service and choose **Restart**.

20. Close the MMC console.

Close any open windows before you begin the next exercise on LON-CL1.

Lab Challenge	Running PowerShell Commands on a Remote Computer
Overview	In this exercise, you will use PowerShell Remoting to connect to a remote computer and execute PowerShell commands.
Mindset	PowerShell Remoting is a server-client application that allows you to securely connect to a remote PowerShell host and run script interactively. It allows you to run commands on a remote system as though you were sitting physically at its console. PowerShell Remoting is built upon the Web Services for Management protocol and uses Windows Remote Management service to handle the authentication and communication elements.
Completion time	15 minutes

1. On **LON-CL1**, click the **Start** button and then type **PowerShell**. From the results, click **Windows PowerShell**. The Windows PowerShell window opens (see Figure 10-4).

Figure 10-4
Opening Windows PowerShell

2. At the Windows PowerShell window, execute the **ps** command.

3. On **LON-CL1**, take a screen shot showing the Windows PowerShell window by pressing **Alt+PrtScr** and then paste it into your Lab10_worksheet file in the page provided by pressing **Ctrl+V**.

4. On CL2, click the **Start** button and then type **PowerShell**. From the results, click **Windows PowerShell**.

5. From the Windows PowerShell window, type **Enable-PSRemoting** and then press **Enter**.

Question 8	Which service is started when you run the Enable-PSRemoting command?

6. On **LON-CL2**, take a screen shot showing the Windows PowerShell window by pressing **Alt+PrtScr** and then paste it into your Lab10_worksheet file in the page provided by pressing **Ctrl+V**.

7. On **LON-CL1**, from the Windows PowerShell window, type the following and press Enter:

   ```
   enter-pssession –ComputerName LON-CL2
   ```

8. Type **ps** and then press **Enter** to see the services running on the LON-CL2.

9. Type **get-service** and then press **Enter** to see the services running on the LON-CL2.

10. Type **get-acl c:** and then press **Enter** to see the access control list applied via NTFS for the C: drive.

11. On **LON-CL1**, take a screen shot showing the Windows PowerShell window by pressing **Alt+PrtScr** and then paste it into your Lab10_worksheet file in the page provided by pressing **Ctrl+V**.

12. Type **exit-pssession** and then press **Enter.**

13. Exit PowerShell by typing **Exit** and pressing **Enter**.

14. Close all windows on LON-CL1 and LON-CL4.

End of lab.

LAB 11
CONFIGURING UPDATES

THIS LAB CONTAINS THE FOLLOWING EXERCISES AND ACTIVITIES:

Exercise 11.1   Configuring Windows 10 Updates

Lab Challenge   Configuring Windows Update Policies

BEFORE YOU BEGIN

The lab environment consists of student workstations connected to a local area network, along with a server that functions as the domain controller for a domain called adatum.com. The computers required for this lab are listed in Table 11-1.

Table 11-1
Computers required for Lab 11

Computer	Operating System	Computer Name
Server (VM 1)	Windows Server 2012 R2	LON-DC1
Client (VM 2)	Windows 10	LON-CL1

In addition to the computers, you will also require the software listed in Table 11-2 to complete Lab 11.

Table 11-2
Software required for Lab 11

Software	Location
Lab 11 student worksheet	Lab11_worksheet.docx (provided by instructor)

Working with Lab Worksheets

Each lab in this manual requires that you answer questions, shoot screen shots, and perform other activities that you will document in a worksheet named for the lab, such as Lab11_worksheet.docx. You will find these worksheets on the book companion site. It is recommended that you use a USB flash drive to store your worksheets, so you can submit them to your instructor for review. As you perform the exercises in each lab, open the appropriate worksheet file, fill in the required information, and then save the file to your flash drive.

SCENARIO

After completing this lab, you will be able to:

■ Configure Windows 10 updates

■ Configure Windows update policies

Estimated lab time: 35 minutes

Exercise 11.1	Configuring Windows 10 Updates
Overview	In this exercise, you will configure Windows 10 updates and then review updates that already been installed.
Mindset	Windows Update provides your Windows 10 users with a way to keep their computers current by checking a designated server. The server provides software that patches security issues, installs updates that make Windows and your applications more stable, fixes issues with existing Windows programs, and provides new features.
Completion time	15 minutes

1. Log on to **LON-CL1** as **adatum\administrator** with the password of **Pa$$w0rd**.

2. Click the **Start** button and then click **Settings**.

3. On the Settings page, click **Update & security**. The Windows Update page opens (see Figure 11-1).

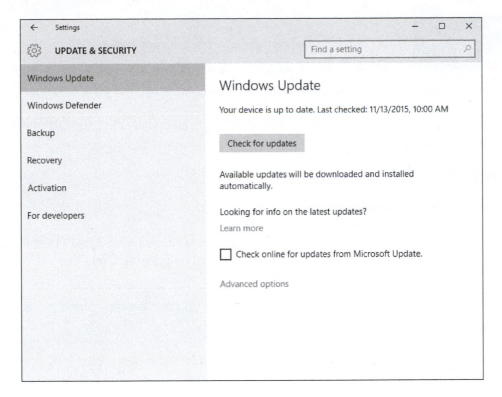

Figure 11-1
Managing Windows updates

Question 1	When was the last time the system was updated?
Question 2	Does the date the system was last updated pose any potential problems?

4. Click **Check for updates**.

Question 3	Did the updates work?

5. Click the **Advanced options** option.

6. Select the **Give me updates for other Microsoft products when I update Windows** option.

Question 4	Which other products would be updated by this option?

Question 5	Which option is selected for how updates are installed?

7. Select the **Choose how updates are delivered** option.

8. To get updates from nearby computers that already got an update, click the **Off** option. It should change to On.

9. Click the **Back** button.

10. Click the **View your update history** option.

11. Take a screen shot of the View Your Update History page by pressing **Alt+PrtScr** and then paste it into your Lab11_worksheet file in the page provided by pressing **Ctrl+V**.

Question 6	What can be used to control which updates are distributed to your corporate clients running Windows 10?

Lab Challenge	Configuring Windows Update Policies
Overview	In this exercise, you will create a Group Policy Object (GPO) that will configure Windows update settings for domain systems.
Mindset	Normally, you do not need to create a domain GPO to support Configuration Manager software updates. However, when you use a GPO to perform a Configuration Manager client agent installation, you must also configure the Windows Update server update options for clients to use the active software update point.
Completion time	20 minutes

1. Log on to **LON-DC1** as **adatum\administrator** with the password of **Pa$$w0rd**.

2. In the Server Manager console, click **Tools > Group Policy Management**.

3. Right-click the **Group Policy Objects** folder (as shown in Figure 11-2) and choose **New**.

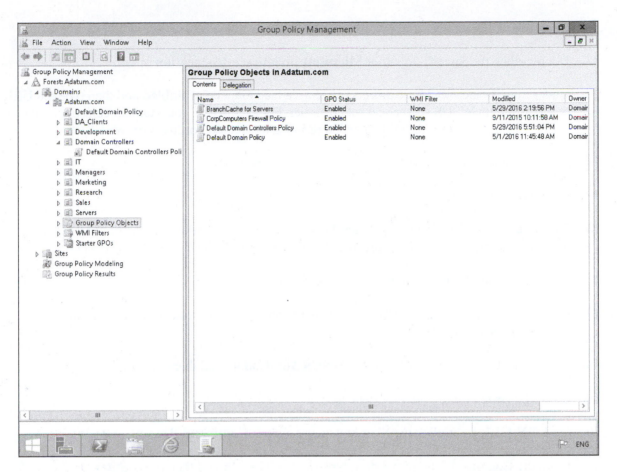

Figure 11-2
Managing GPOs

4. In the Name field, type **WSUS AutoUpdate** and then click **OK**.

5. Expand the Group Policy Objects folder and then right-click the **WSUS AutoUpdate** GPO and choose **Edit**.

6. In the Group Policy Management Editor, expand **Computer Configuration > Policies > Administrative Templates > Windows Components > Windows Update**.

7. In the details pane, double-click **Configure Automatic Updates**.

8. Under Configure Automatic Updates, click **Enabled**. Under Configure Automatic updating, review the options.

9. Under Configure automatic updating, make sure **3 - Auto download and notify for install** is visible. Read the information in the help panel to understand how this setting works.

Question 7	What is the scheduled install time?

10. Click **OK**.

11. Double-click the **Specify intranet Microsoft update service location** option.

12. Under Specify intranet Microsoft update service location, click **Enabled** and then type the URL of the upstream WSUS server you set up earlier. For example, if your domain controller's name is LON-DC1, type http://LON-DC1:8530 (8530 is the default port used by WSUS).

13. For the intranet statistics server, type the same information.

14. Click **OK**.

15. Take a screen shot of the Group Policy Management Editor window by pressing **Alt+PrtScr** and then paste it into your Lab11_worksheet file in the page provided by pressing **Ctrl+V**.

16. Close the Group Policy Management Editor window.

17. Back in the Group Policy Management console, right-click the **Adatum.com** node and choose **Link an existing GPO**.

18. In the Select GPO dialog box, choose **WSUS AutoUpdate** and then click **OK**.

19. Close the Group Policy Management console.

20. On **LON-CL1**, right-click the Start button and choose **Command Prompt (Admin)**.

21. From the Command Prompt window, type **gpresult /r** and then press **Enter**.

22. The WSUS AutoUpdate GPO should appear under the **Computer Settings > Applied Group Policy Objects** section of the report. If it does not, type **gpupdate /force** and then try **gpresult /r** again.

23. Type **wuauclt /detectnow** and then press **Enter**. This forces the Windows 10 computer to contact the WSUS server immediately.

24. Close all windows.

End of lab.

LAB 12
MONITORING WINDOWS

THIS LAB CONTAINS THE FOLLOWING EXERCISES AND ACTIVITIES:

Exercise 12.1 Using Event Viewer

Exercise 12.2 Using Reliability Monitor

Exercise 12.3 Using Task Manager

Exercise 12.4 Using Resource Monitor

Exercise 12.5 Using Performance Monitor

Lab Challenge Configuring Indexing Options

BEFORE YOU BEGIN

The lab environment consists of student workstations connected to a local area network, along with a server that functions as the domain controller for a domain called adatum.com. The computers required for this lab are listed in Table 12-1.

Table 12-1
Computers required for Lab12

Computer	Operating System	Computer Name
Server (VM 1)	Windows Server 2012 R2	LON-DC1
Client (VM 2)	Windows 10	LON-CL1
Client (VM 3)	Windows 10	LON-CL2

In addition to the computers, you will also require the software listed in Table 12-2 to complete Lab 12.

Table 12-2
Software required for Lab 12

Software	Location
Lab 12 student worksheet	Lab12_worksheet.docx (provided by instructor)

Working with Lab Worksheets

Each lab in this manual requires that you answer questions, shoot screen shots, and perform other activities that you will document in a worksheet named for the lab, such as Lab12_worksheet.docx. You will find these worksheets on the book companion site. It is recommended that you use a USB flash drive to store your worksheets, so you can submit them to your instructor for review. As you perform the exercises in each lab, open the appropriate worksheet file, fill in the required information, and then save the file to your flash drive.

SCENARIO

After completing this lab, you will be able to:

- Use Event Viewer

- Use Reliability Monitor

- Use Task Manager

- Use Resource Monitor

- Use Performance Monitor

- Configure indexing options

Estimated lab time: 120 minutes

Exercise 12.1	Using Event Viewer
Overview	In this exercise, you will use Event Viewer to view the events stored in the Windows logs. Because there can be thousands of log entries, you learn how to filter the logs to show only what you need to focus on. You also learn how to set up subscriptions to consolidate the logs onto one server.
Mindset	The Event Viewer is an MMC snap-in that enables you to browse and manage event logs. It is included in the Computer Management console and is included in Administrative Tools as a stand-alone console. You can also execute the eventvwr.msc command.
Completion time	40 minutes

Looking at Events

1. Log on to LON-CL1 using the **Administrator** account and the **Pa$$w0rd** password.

2. Right-click the **Start** button and choose **Event Viewer**. In the Event Viewer, expand the Event Window to fill up the screen, as shown in Figure 12-1.

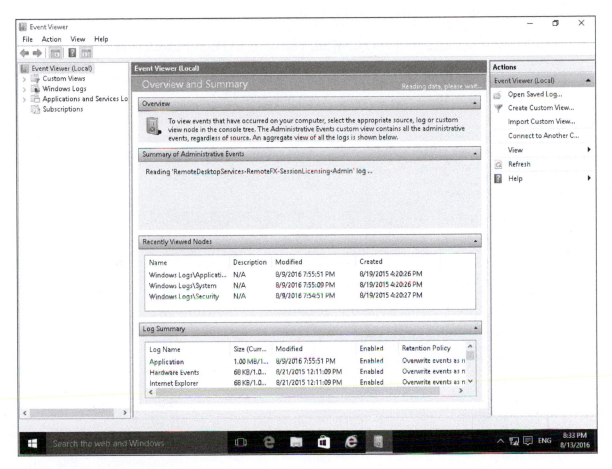

Figure 12-1
Opening Event Viewer

3. Expand the **Windows Logs** folder and then click the **System** log. The contents of the log appear in the detail pane.

Question 1	*How many events appear in the System log?*

4. Click **Action > Filter Current Log**. The Filter Current Log dialog box appears.

5. In the Event Level area, select the **Critical**, **Warning,** and **Error** check boxes. Then click **OK**.

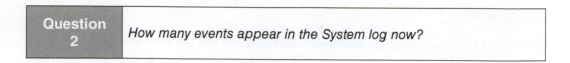

Question 2	*How many events appear in the System log now?*

6. Click **Action > Create Custom View**. The Create Custom View dialog box appears.

7. In the Logged drop-down list, select **Last 7 days**.

8. In the Event Level area, select the **Critical**, **Warning**, and **Error** check boxes.

9. Leave the By log option selected and, in the Event logs drop-down list, select the **Application**, **Security**, and **System** check boxes, as shown in Figure 12-2.

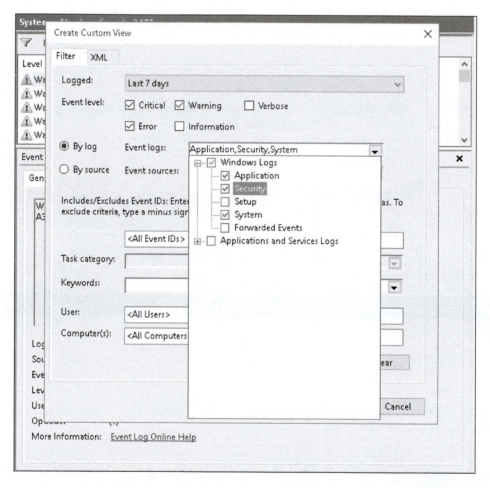

Figure 12-2
Selecting the types of logs

10. Click **OK**. The Save Filter to Custom View dialog box appears.

11. In the Name text box, type **Critical, Warning & Error**. Then click **OK**. The Critical, Warning & Error view you just created appears in the Custom Views folder.

Question 3	*How many events appear in the Critical, Warning & Error custom view?*

12. Take a screen shot of the Critical, Warning & Error view by pressing **Alt+PrtScr** and then paste it into your Lab12_worksheet file in the page provided by pressing **Ctrl+V**.

13. Right-click **System** (under Windows Logs) and choose **Clear Filter**.

Leave the Event Viewer console open for the next exercise.

Adding a Task to an Event

1. On **LON-CL1**, using Event Viewer, click the **Application** log.

2. In the Application logs, find a Windows Error Reporting information event (event 1001). Then right-click the event 1001 and choose **Attach Task to This Event**, as shown in Figure 12-3.

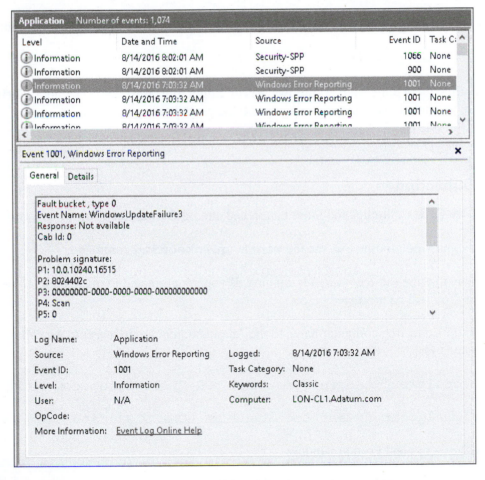

Figure 12-3
Attaching a task to an event

3. In the Create a Basic Task Wizard, click **Next**.

4. On the When a Specified Event Is Logged page, click **Next**.

5. On the Action page, make sure Start a program is selected and then click **Next**.

6. On the Start a Program page, in the Program/script text box, type **Notepad**. Click **Next**.

7. On the Summary page, click **Finish**.

8. In the Event Viewer dialog box, take a screen shot showing the Event Viewer/scheduled task application by pressing **Alt+PrtScr** and then paste it into your Lab12_worksheet file in the page provided by pressing **Ctrl+V**.

9. Click **OK**.

10. Click the Start button and then type **Task Scheduler**. From the search results, click **Task Scheduler**.

11. In Task Scheduler, expand the Task Scheduler Library and then click the **Event Viewer Tasks** node.

12. Right-click the **Application_Windows_Error Reporting_1001** task and choose **Run**.

13. When Notepad opens, close it.

14. Right-click the **Application_Windows_Error Reporting_1001** task and choose **Delete**. When you are prompted to confirm that you want to delete this task, click **Yes**.

15. Close **Task Scheduler**.

Creating a Subscription

1. On **LON-CL1**, right-click the **Start** button and choose **Command Prompt** (**Admin**).

2. At the command prompt, execute the `winrm quickconfig` command.

   It is okay that the service is already running. If you are prompted to make these changes, click **Y** for Yes. You will be prompted twice.

3. To add the collecting computer name to the Administrators group, execute the following commands:

   ```
   net localgroup "Administrators" LON-CL2$@adatum.com /add

   net localgroup "Event Log Readers" LON-CL2$@adatum.com /add
   ```

4. Close the Command Prompt window.

5. Right-click the **Start** button and choose **Event Viewer**.

6. Click **Subscriptions**. When you are prompted to confirm that you want to start the service and configure the service to automatically start, click **Yes**.

7. Log on to **LON-CL2** as **adatum\administrator** and the **Pa$$w0rd** password.

8. On **LON-CL2**, right-click **Start** and choose **Command Prompt (Admin)**.

9. On **LON-CL2**, at the command prompt, execute the `wecutil qc` command.

    If you are prompted to confirm that you would like to proceed, type **Y** and press **Enter**.

10. Close the Command Prompt window.

11. On **LON-CL2**, right-click the Start button and choose **Event Viewer**.

12. Click and then right-click **Subscriptions** and choose **Create Subscription**. The Subscription Properties dialog box opens.

13. In the Subscription name text box, type **LON-CL1**.

14. Click the **Select Computers** button. The Computers dialog box opens.

15. Click the **Add Domain Computers** button. In the Enter the object name to select text box, type **LON-CL1** and click **OK**.

16. Close the Computers dialog box by clicking **OK**.

17. Click the **Select Events** button. The Query Filter dialog box opens.

18. For the Event level, select **Critical**, **Warning**, **Error,** and **Information**.

19. For Event Logs, click **Application**, **Security**, and **System** logs.

20. Close the Query filter dialog box by clicking **OK**.

21. Close the Subscription Properties dialog box by clicking **OK**.

22. Take a screen shot showing the Subscriptions node by pressing **Alt+PrtScr** and then paste it into your Lab12_worksheet file in the page provided by pressing **Ctrl+V**.

23. On **LON-CL2**, in Event Viewer, under Windows Logs, click **Forwarded Events**. Remember that events are not displayed immediately.

Question 4	*Do you see any events? If events do not appear, which Windows component could block the packets from being received by the collector computer?*

24. On LON-CL1, right-click the **Start** button and choose **Control Panel**. Then click **System and Security > Windows Firewall**.

25. Click the **Turn Windows Firewall on or off** option. For the Domain network settings, select the **Turn off Windows Firewall** option and then click **OK**.

26. On LON-CL2, right-click the **Start** button and choose **Control Panel**. Then click **System and Security > Windows Firewall**.

27. Click the **Turn Windows Firewall on or off** option. For the Domain network settings, select the **Turn off Windows Firewall** option and then click **OK**.

28. On **LON-CL2**, every minute or so, right-click the **Forwarded Events** node and choose **Refresh**,. You should begin seeing events within a couple of minutes. If you don't see any events in the Forwarded Events, you return to LON-CL2 and look in Event Viewer's Forwarded Events node to view the forwarded events.

29. After events are shown in the Forwarded Events node, click the **Subscription** node.

30. Right-click the LON-CL2 subscription and choose **Delete**. When you are prompted to confirm this action, click **Yes**.

Close any open windows on LON-CL1 and LON-CL2 before you begin the next exercise.

Exercise 12.2	Using Reliability Monitor
Overview	Reliability Monitor is a hidden tool that can determine the reliability of a system, including allowing you to see whether any recent changes have been made to the system itself. During this exercise, you will open Reliability Monitor to check the status of the computer.
Mindset	Reliability Monitor is a Control Panel/Action Panel tool that measures hardware and software problems and other changes to your computer that could affect the reliability of the computer.
Completion time	10 minutes

1. On **LON-CL1**, click the Start Menu. Type **perfmon /rel** and then press **Enter**. Reliability Monitor opens.

2. Take a screen shot of the Reliability Monitor page by pressing **Alt+PrtScr** and then paste it into your Lab12_worksheet file in the page provided by pressing **Ctrl+V**.

3. At the bottom of the screen, click **View all problem reports**.

Question 5	Are any problems reported?

4. Close the Problem reports window by clicking **OK**.

5. Close Reliability Monitor by clicking **OK**.

Leave LON-CL1 open on for the next exercise.

Exercise 12.3	Using Task Manager
Overview	In this exercise, you will use Task Manager to look at the primary performance systems. In addition, you will view and manage running processes.
Mindset	Task Manager is one of the handiest programs you can use to take a quick glance at performance to see which programs are using the most system resources on your computer. You can see the status of running programs and programs that have stopped responding You can also stop a program running in memory.
Completion time	20 minutes

1. On LON-CL1, right-click the **Taskbar** and choose **Task Manager**.

Question 6	Which applications are running?

Question 7	Which tabs are shown?

2. Click **More Details**.

Question 8	Which tabs are shown?

3. Open **WordPad** by clicking the Start button, typing **WordPad**, and from the results, clicking **Wordpad**.

Question 9	In the Apps section, which processes are used for Wordpad?

4. On Task Manager, click **Fewer details**.

5. Right-click **Windows Wordpad Application** and choose **End Task**.

6. Start **WordPad** again.

7. On Task Manager, click **More details**.

8. Right-click **Windows Wordpad Application** and choose **Open file location**.

Question 10	*Where was the wordpad.exe file located?*

9. Close the **Accessories** folder.

Question 11	*How much memory is being used by Wordpad?*

10. Right-click the **Name** title at the top of the first column and choose **Process name** (see Figure 12-4).

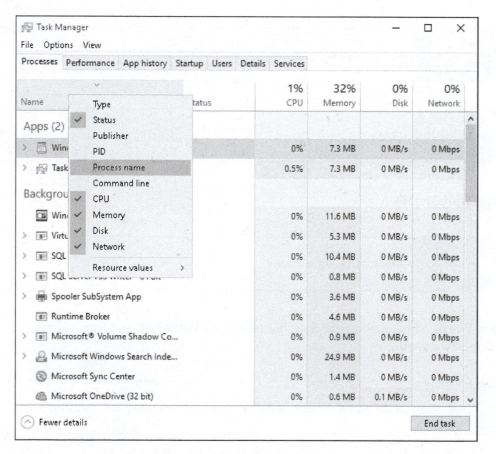

Figure 12-4
Adding the Process name so that it can also be displayed

11. Right-click **Windows WordPad Application** and choose **End Task**.

12. Click the **Performance** tab.

Question 12	*What are the primary systems that you can monitor with Task Manager?*

Question 13	*How many virtual processors are being used by LON-CL1?*

13. Click **Memory** and **Ethernet** to view what each option has to offer.

14. Click the **Users** tab.

15. Expand **Administrator** to display the programs and processes being executed by the administrator.

16. To see a detailed list of all processes running, click the **Details** tab.

17. To display additional columns, right-click the **Name** column title and choose **Select columns**.

18. In the Select columns dialog box, click to select **Session ID** and **Threads**. Click **OK**.

19. Take a screen shot of the Task Manager window by pressing **Alt+PrtScr** and then paste it into your Lab12_worksheet file in the page provided by pressing **Ctrl+V**.

20. To sort by components that make up the most memory, click the **Memory (private work set)** title.

21. From time to time, a program or action might cause Windows Explorer to stop functioning. In these cases, you can use Task Manager to stop and restart Explorer. Therefore, find and right-click **explorer.exe** and then choose **End task**. When you are prompted to confirm that you want to end explorer.exe, click **End process**.

22. Click **File > Run new task**.

23. In the Create new task dialog box, in the Open text box, type **explorer** and then click **OK**.

24. To view the current services, click the **Services** tab.

On LON-CL1, close Task Manager.

Exercise 12.4	Using Resource Monitor
Overview	In this exercise, you will use Resource Manager to monitor server resources.
Mindset	Resource Monitor is a system tool that allows you to view information about the use of hardware (CPU, memory, disk, and network) and software resources (file handlers and modules) in real time.
Completion time	10 minutes

1. On LON-CL1, click the **Start** button, type **resource monitor**, and then press **Enter**. Maximimize the Resource Monitor window.

Question 14	Which systems can be monitored with Resource Monitor?

2. Click the **CPU** tab.

3. To sort the processes alphabetically, click the **Image** header.

4. Take a screen shot of the Resource Monitor window by pressing **Alt+PrtScr** and then paste it into your Lab12_worksheet file in the page provided by pressing **Ctrl+V**.

5. Click the **Memory** tab and then click the Working Set (KB) column to sort memory usage.

Question 15	Which process is using the most memory?

6. Click the **Disk** tab.

Question 16	Which process is using the disk the most?

7. Click the **Network** tab and then expand **TCP Connections**.

Question 17	Which local port is being used by svchost.exe (NetworkService)?

8. Close **Resource Monitor**.

Leave LON-CL1 open for the next exercise.

Exercise 12.5	Using Performance Monitor
Overview	Although Task Manager and Resource Manager gave you a quick look at your system performance, Performance Monitor allows you to thoroughly exam the performance of a system. In this exercise, you will open Performance Monitor and show various counters.
Mindset	Performance Monitor is an MMC snap-in that provides tools for analyzing system performance. From a single console, you can monitor application and hardware performance in real time, specify which data you want to collect in logs, define thresholds for alerts and automatic actions, generate reports, and view past performance data in a variety of ways.
Completion time	30 minutes

Using Counters with Performance Monitor

1. On **LON-CL1**, click **Start**, type **Performance Monitor**, and then press **Enter**.

2. Browse to and click **Monitoring Tools\Performance Monitor**.

3. Click **% Processor Time** at the bottom of the screen. To remove the counter, click the **Delete (red X)** button at the top of the Window.

4. Click the **Add** (green plus (+) sign) button in the toolbar. The Add Counters dialog box appears.

5. Under Available counters, expand **Processor**, click **% Processor Time**, and then click **Show description**, as shown in Figure 12-5. Read the description for % Processor Time.

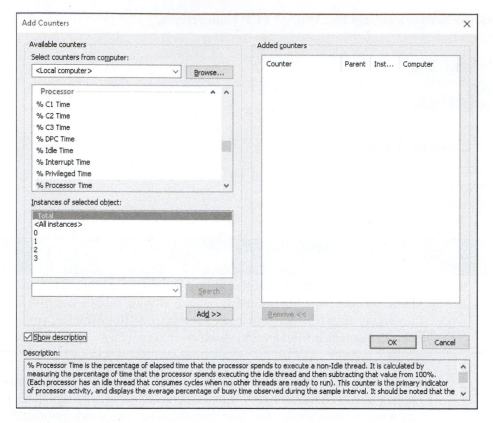

Figure 12-5
Looking at a description of a counter

6. Click **Add**. % Processor Time should show up in the Added counters section.

7. Under Available Counters, expand the **Server Work Queues** and then click the **Queue Length** counter. Under Instances of selected objects, click **0**. Then click **Add**.

8. Add the following counters:

   • System: **Processor Queue Length**

   • Memory: **Page Faults/Sec**

   • Memory: **Pages/Sec**

   • PhysicalDisk (**_Total**): **Current Disk Queue Length**

9. Click **OK** to close the Add Counters dialog box.

10. At the top of the graph, a toolbar with 13 buttons is displayed. Click the down arrow of the **Change graph type** (third button) and then click **Histogram bar**.

11. Change the graph type to **Report**.

12. Change back to the **Line graph**.

13. Click the **Properties** button (the fourth button from the end) on the toolbar. The Performance Monitor Properties sheet appears. Notice the counters that you have selected.

14. Click **Processor (_Total)\%Processor Time**.

15. Change the width to heaviest line width. Change the color to **Red**.

16. Click the **Graph** tab.

17. In the Vertical scale box, change the value of the Maximum field to **200** and then click **OK**.

18. Take a screen shot of the Performance Monitor window by pressing **Alt+PrtScr** and then paste it into your Lab12_worksheet file in the page provided by pressing **Ctrl+V**.

Using DCS

1. On **LON-CL1**, in the left pane, expand **Data Collector Sets**.

2. Right-click the **User Defined** folder and choose **New > Data Collector Set**. In the Name: text box, type **MyDCS**.

3. Click **Create manually (Advanced)** and then click **Next**.

4. When you are prompted to choose the type of data you want to include, select **Performance Counter** and then click **Next**.

5. To add counters, click **Add**.

6. Under Available Counters, expand the **Processor** node by clicking the down arrow next to Processor. Scroll down and click **%Processor Time**. Click **Add**.

7. Add the following counters.

   - Server Work Queues: **Queue Length**

   - System: **Processor Queue Length**

   - Memory: **Page Faults/Sec**

   - Memory: **Pages/Sec**

   - PhysicalDisk (_Total): **Current Disk Queue Length**

8. Click **OK** and then click **Next**.

9. Click **Finish**.

10. Right-click **MyDCS** and choose **Start**.

11. Let it run for at least two minutes.

12. Right-click **MyDCS** and choose **Stop**.

13. Open File Explorer and navigate to **c:\PerfLogs\Admin\MyDCS**. Then open the folder that was just created.

14. Double-click **DataCollector01.blg**. The Performance Monitor graph opens.

Question 18	*Now that the DCS has been created, what advantages are provided by MyDCS?*

15. Take a screen shot of the Performance Monitor window by pressing **Alt+PrtScr** and then paste it into your Lab12_worksheet file in the page provided by pressing **Ctrl+V**.

16. Close the Performance Monitor graph and the MyDCS folder.

17. Close **Performance Monitor**.

Leave LON-CL1 open for the next exercise.

Lab Challenge	Configuring Indexing Options
Overview	In this exercise, you will view and configure the indexing options on a computer running Windows 10.
Mindset	Windows can have hundreds or even thousands of data files spread through multiple folders or even drives. When you have this many files, you don't necessarily know where each file is. To make your searches go smoothly and quickly, you must index your data documents. When files are not indexed properly, you might need a long time to search for a file; you also might have trouble finding the file that you seek.
Completion time	10 minutes

1. On **LON-CL1**, click the **Start** button and type **index**. From the results, click **Indexing Options**.

2. In the Indexing Options dialog box (see Figure 12-6), click **Modify**.

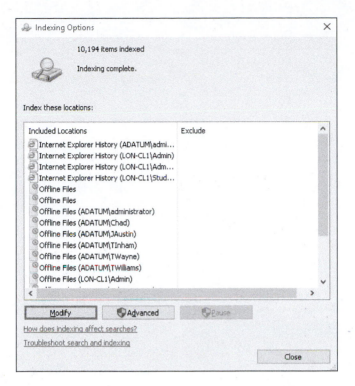

Figure 12-6
Managing indexing options

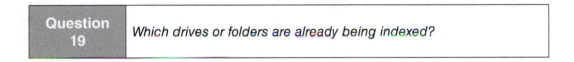

Question 19	*Which drives or folders are already being indexed?*

3. Select the **Local Disk (C:)** and then click **OK**.

4. Click the **Advanced** button.

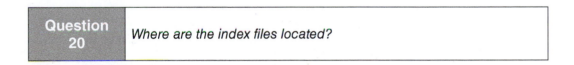

Question 20	*Where are the index files located?*

5. To rebuild the index, click the **Rebuild** button. When a message indicates that the index might take a long time to complete, click **OK**.

6. Take a screen shot of the Indexing Options window by pressing **Alt+PrtScr** and then paste it into your Lab12_worksheet file in the page provided by pressing **Ctrl+V**.

7. Close the Indexing Options dialog box by clicking **Close**.

8. Log off LON-CL1 and LON-CL2.

End of lab.

LAB 13
CONFIGURING SYSTEM AND DATA RECOVERY

THIS LAB CONTAINS THE FOLLOWING EXERCISES AND ACTIVITIES:

Exercise 13.1   Configuring Windows Defender

Exercise 13.2   Configuring a Restore Point

Exercise 13.3   Scheduling a Windows 10 Backup

Exercise 13.4   Performing a File Restore

Exercise 13.5   Using File History

Lab Challenge   Recovering Files from OneDrive

BEFORE YOU BEGIN

The lab environment consists of student workstations connected to a local area network, along with a server that functions as the domain controller for a domain called adatum.com. The computers required for this lab are listed in Table 13-1.

Table 13-1
Computers required for Lab 13

Computer	Operating System	Computer Name
Server (VM 1)	Windows Server 2012 R2	LON-DC1
Client (VM 2)	Windows 10	LON-CL1

In addition to the computers, you will also require the software listed in Table 13-2 to complete Lab 13.

Table 13-2
Software required for Lab 13

Software	Location
Lab 13 student worksheet	Lab13_worksheet.docx (provided by instructor)

Working with Lab Worksheets

Each lab in this manual requires that you answer questions, shoot screen shots, and perform other activities that you will document in a worksheet named for the lab, such as Lab13_worksheet.docx. You will find these worksheets on the book companion site. It is recommended that you use a USB flash drive to store your worksheets, so you can submit them to your instructor for review. As you perform the exercises in each lab, open the appropriate worksheet file, fill in the required information, and then save the file to your flash drive.

SCENARIO

After completing this lab, you will be able to:

■ Configure Windows Defender

■ Configure a restore point

■ Perform a file restore

■ Configure file history

■ Recover files with OneDrive

Estimated lab time: 100 minutes

Exercise 13.1	Configuring Windows Defender
Overview	In this exercise, you will open Windows Defender and initiate a quick scan. You will then configure Windows Defender settings and schedule a scan.
Mindset	Windows Defender is designed to protect your computer against viruses, spyware, and other types of malware. It protects against these threats by providing real-time protection in which it notifies you if malware attempts to install itself on your computer or when an application tries to change critical settings.
Completion time	20 minutes

1. Log on to **LON-CL1** as **adatum\administrator** with the password of **Pa$$w0rd**.

2. Click the **Start** button and then type **Defender**. Then from the results, click **Windows Defender**. Windows Defender opens. After a couple of minutes, Windows Defender will indicate the PC is Potentially unprotected, as shown in Figure 13-1.

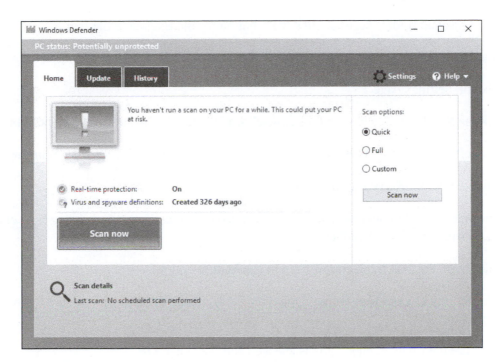

Figure 13-1
Windows Defender

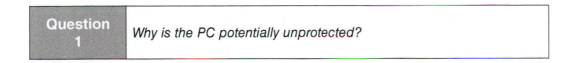

Question 1	Why is the PC potentially unprotected?

3. Click the **Update** tab and then click the **Update definitions** button.

4. If the system does not have have Internet access, it will not be able to perform an update. Therefore, click the **Cancel update** button.

5. Click the **Home** tab.

6. With the Quick scan option selected, click the **Scan now** button.

7. When the scan is complete, click the **Settings** option. The Settings Windows Defender page opens.

Question 2	What is the real-time protection set to?

Question 3	*What is the cloud-based protection set to?*

8. In the Exclusions section, click **Add an exclusion** option.

9. In the Files and folders section, click the **+** button for the Exclude a file button.

10. In the Open text box, type **C:\BOOTNXT** and then click the **Exclude this file** button.

11. Close the Settings page.

12. Click the **Start** button and then type **taskschd.msc**. From the results, click **Task Scheduler**.

13. In the left pane, expand **Task Scheduler Library > Microsoft > Windows > Windows Defender**.

14. Double-click **Windows Defender Scheduled Scan** task.

15. In the Windows Defender Scheduled Scan Properties (Local Computer) dialog box, click the **Triggers** tab and then click **New**.

16. In the Begin the task field, choose the **On a schedule** option.

17. Under Settings, select **One time**. In the Start field, change the time to 3 minutes from your current time.

18. Make sure the Enabled check box is checked and then click **OK**.

19. Close the Windows Defender Scheduled Scan Properties dialog box by clicking **OK**.

20. Take a screen shot of Task Manager showing the Windows Defender Scheduled Scan task by pressing **Alt+PrtScr** and then paste it into your Lab13_worksheet file in the page provided by pressing **Ctrl+V**.

Leave LON-CL1 open for the next exercise.

Exercise 13.2	Configuring a Restore Point
Overview	In this exercise, you will create a restore point that can be used to roll back to a previous state.
Mindset	Sometimes when you install an application or perform an upgrade, the installation or upgrade causes major problems with Windows. In these situations, you can use a restore point to restore the system to its original state before the ugprade.
Completion time	20 minutes

1. On **LON-CL1**, right-click the **Start** button and choose **Control Panel**.

2. In the Search Control Panel text box, type **Create a Restore point**. Under System, click **Create a restore point**. The System Properties dialog box displays (see Figure 13-2).

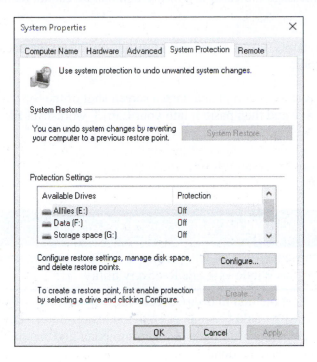

Figure 13-2
The System Properties dialog box

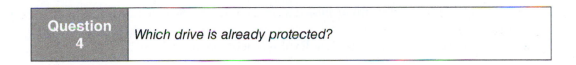

Question 4	*Which drive is already protected?*

3. Click the **Local Disk (C:)** and then click **Configure**.

4. In the System Protection dialog box, click **Turn on system protection**. Click **OK**.

5. To create a restore point, click **Create**.

6. In the System Protection dialog box, in the text box, type **Test** and then click **Create**.

7. When the restore point is created, take a screen shot of the The restore point was created successfully message by pressing **Alt+Prt Scr** and then paste it into your Lab13_worksheet file in the page provided by pressing **Ctrl+V**.

8. Click **Close**.

9. In the System Properties dialog box, click **System Restore**.

10. On the System Restore Wizard page, click **Next**.

11. When a list of current restore points is displayed, click the **Test** restore point that you just made and then click **Next**.

12. On the Confirm your restore point page, click **Finish**.

13. When a warning message indicates that the system restore cannot be interrupted, click **Yes** to continue.

14. After LON-CL1 reboots, log on using the **adatum\administrator** account and the **Pa$$w0rd** password.

15. When the system restore is completed, take a screen shot of the System Restore dialog box by pressing **Alt+Prt Scr** and then paste it into your Lab13_worksheet file in the page provided by pressing **Ctrl+V**.

16. Click **Close** to close the System Restore dialog box.

Exercise 13.3	Scheduling a Windows 10 Backup
Overview	In this exercise, you will perform a backup and then schedule a backup using the Windows 7 File Recovery utility.
Mindset	The best method in disaster recovery is to have a good backup. A disaster could be small or could be major. But if you have a backup of your data, you can restore to a computer and continue with the work that needs to be done.
Completion time	30 minutes

1. Log on to **LON-DC1** as **adatum\administrator** with the **Pa$$w0rd** password.

2. Open **File Explorer** by clicking the **File Explorer** icon on the taskbar.

3. Under Computer, click **Local Disk (C:)**.

4. Right-click **Local Disk (C:)** and choose **New > Folder**. For the folder name, type **BAK** and then press **Enter**.

5. Right-click the **C:\BAK** folder and choose **Properties**.

6. In the BAK Properties dialog box, click the **Sharing** tab.

7. Click the **Advanced Sharing** button.

8. In the Advanced Sharing dialog box, click to select the **Share this folder**.

9. Click the **Permissions** button.

10. Click to select **Allow Full Control Permission** for the Everyone group.

11. Click **OK** to close the Permissions for BAK dialog box.

12. Click **OK** to close the Advanced Sharing dialog box.

13. Click **Close** to close the BAK Properties dialog box.

14. Right-click the **Start** button and choose **Control Panel**.

15. In the Search Control Panel text box, type **File Recovery**. On the Windows 7 File Recovery page, click **Backup and Restore (Windows 7)**. The Windows File Recovery page displays (see Figure 13-3).

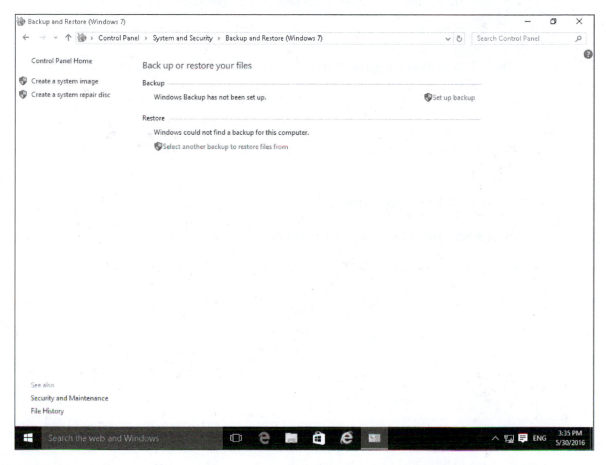

Figure 13-3
The Windows 7 File Recovery page

16. Click **Set up backup**.

17. On the Set up backup page, answer the following question.

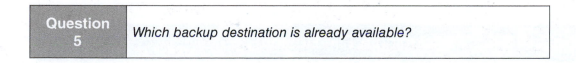

Question 5	Which backup destination is already available?

18. Click **Save on a network**.

19. In the Set up backup page, in the Network location text box, type **\\LON-DC1\BAK**.

20. In the Username text box, type **adatum\administrator**. In the Password text box, type **Pa$$w0rd**. Click **OK**.

21. Back on the Set up backup page, ensure **\\LON-DC1\BAK** is selected and then click **Next**.

22. On the What do you want to back up? page, select **Let me choose** and then click **Next**.

Question 6	By default, which items are selected for backup?

23. Deselect **Include a system image of drives: System Reserved, (C:)** and then click **Next**.

24. On the Review your backup settings page, click **Save settings and run backup**.

25. When the backup finishes, take a screen shot of the Backup and Restore (Windows 7) page by pressing **Alt+Prt Scr** and then paste it into your Lab13_worksheet file in the page provided by pressing **Ctrl+V**.

26. Under Schedule, click **Change settings**.

27. On the Select where you want to save your backup page, click **Next**.

28. On the What do you want to back up? page, click **Next**.

29. On the What do you want to back up? second page, click **Next**.

30. On the Review your backup settings page, click **Change schedule**.

Question 7	When is the backup scheduled?

31. Change the time to **8:00 PM** and then click **OK**.

32. On the Review your backup settings page, take a screen shot by pressing **Alt+Prt Scr** and then paste it into your Lab13_worksheet file in the page provided by pressing **Ctrl+V**.

33. Click **Save settings and exit**.

Leave the Backup and Restore (Windows 7) page open for the next exercise.

Exercise 13.4	Performing a File Restore
Overview	In this exercise, you will restore a file that was backed up last exercise.
Mindset	When you have a backup, you will need to know how to restore files from that backup. As a reminder, you should always test your backups from time to time by performing a restore of some files.
Completion time	10 minutes

1. Answer the following question. Then on **LON-CL1**, using Backup and Restore (Windows 7), under the Restore section, click the **Restore my files** button.

Question 8	*When you want to use the current backup of all of the files, which option should be selected?*

2. On the Restore Files page (see Figure 13-4), click **Browse for folders**.

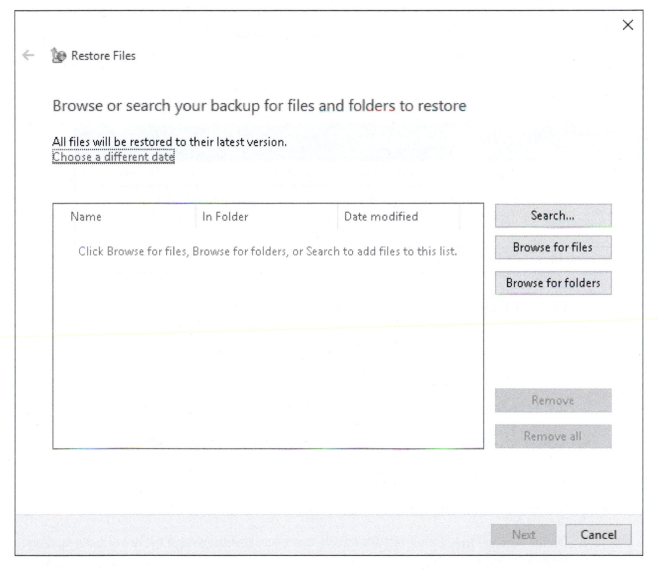

Figure 13-4
The Restore Files page

3. In the Browse the backup for folders or drives dialog box, click **Administrator's backup** and then click **Add folder**.

4. Back on the Browse or search your backup for files and folders to restore page, click **Next**.

5. When you are prompted to identify where you want to restore the files, **In the original location** is already selected. Click **Restore**.

6. In the Copy file dialog box, click to select the **Do this for all conflicts** option and then click **Copy and Replace**.

7. When the restore has been completed, take a screen shot of the Your files have been restored page by pressing **Alt+Prt Scr** and then paste it into your Lab13_worksheet file in the page provided by pressing **Ctrl+V**.

8. Click **Finish**.

9. Turn off automatic backups by clicking the **Turn off schedule** link.

10. Close **Backup and Restore (Windows 7)**.

Exercise 13.5   Using File History

Overview	In this exercise, you will restore a file that is saved in File History.
Mindset	File History periodically makes a copy of a data folder and keeps several copies of those files. Then you can restore the files from File History using any of the saved copies.
Completion time	10 minutes

1. On **LON-CL1**, open File Explorer by clicking **File Explorer** on the tasbar.

2. If you do not have an E drive, use the following steps:

    a. Right-click the **Start** button and choose **Disk Management**. Disk Management opens.

    b. If you are prompted to initialize disks, click **OK**.

    c. Right-click the 10 GB Unallocated disk and choose **New Simple Volume**.

    d. In the New Simple Volume Wizard, on the Welcome screen, click **Next**.

    e. On the Specify Volume Size page, click **Next**.

    f. On the Assign Drive Letter or Path screen, make sure that the assign the driver letter is **E** and then click **Next**.

    g. On the Format Partition screen, in the Volume label text box, type **Data**. Click **Next**.

    h. On the Completing the New Simple Volume Wizard screen, click **Finish**.

    i. When a Microsoft Windows dialog box opens asking to format the disk, click **Cancel**.

j. Close the File Explorer Data (E:) window.

k. Close **Disk Manager** and then close the other **File Explorer**.

3. On **LON-CL1**, right-click the desktop and choose **New > Text Document**. Name the document **Test**.

4. Right-click the **Start** button and choose **Control Panel**.

5. In the Search Control Panel text box, type **File History**. When the File History option is displayed, click **File History**. The File History page displays (see Figure 13-5).

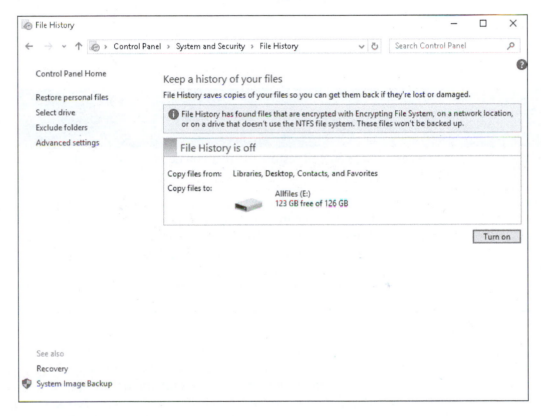

Figure 13-5
The File History page

6. Click the **Turn on** button.

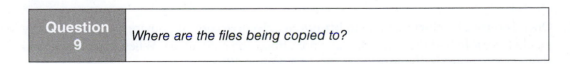

Question 9	*Where are the files being copied to?*

7. After a few seconds, click **Run now**.

8. Take a screen shot of the File History page by pressing **Alt+Prt Scr** and then paste it into your Lab13_worksheet file in the page provided by pressing **Ctrl+V**.

9. In the left pane, click **Restore personal files**.

10. In the Home - File History window, double-click **Desktop**.

11. Click **Test** and, at the bottom of the window, click the (green) **Restore to original location** button.

12. In the Replace or Skip Files dialog box, click **Replace the file in the destination**.

13. Close the **Desktop** window.

14. Close the **Desktop - File History** dialog box.

15. Close the **File History** window.

Lab Challenge	Recovering Files from OneDrive
Overview	In this exercise, you will restore file that you delete in Microsoft OneDrive.
Mindset	OneDrive is a file-hosting service that allows you to store and create files and folders and share them with other users and groups. Similar to deleting local files in Windows 10, if you accidentally delete a file, you have 30 days to recover from the OneDrive Recycle Bin (a temporary storage place of deleted items).
Completion time	10 minutes

> **NOTE**
>
> *You will not be able to perform this exercise on the MOAC Labs Online systems. Instead, you need to use a computer running Windows 10 with access to the Internet. If your classroom has a dedicated Windows Server 2012 R2 or Windows Server 2016, you can use a virtual machine running Windows 10.*

1. Log on to a Windows 10 computer that is connected to the Internet.

2. Open **Internet Explorer** and go to **http://onedrive.live.com**. If you are not automatically logged in, click **Sign In** and then sign in with your Office 365 credentials. When you are logged in, you should see a page similar to what is shown in Figure 13-6.

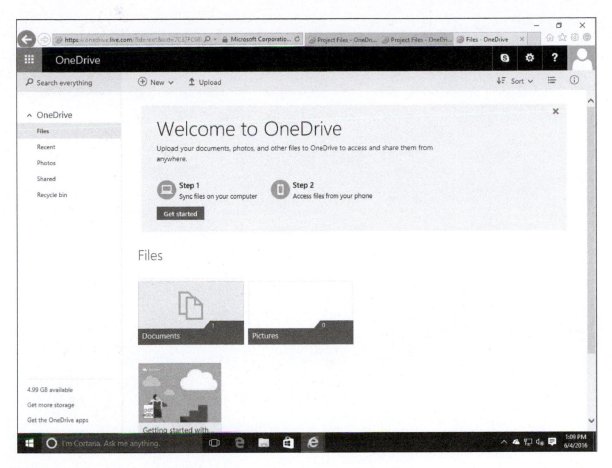

Figure 13-6
The OneDrive web page

3. Click the **Documents** folder and then click the **Project Files** folder.

4. Right-click the Project Scope.docx file and choose **Delete**.

5. Click the **Recycle bin** link.

6. Right-click a ProjectScope.docx document and choose **Restore**.

7. Navigate back to the Project Files folder; you will see the document.

8. Take a screen shot of the OneDrive page by pressing **Alt+Prt Scr** and then paste it into your Lab13_worksheet file in the page provided by pressing **Ctrl+V**.

9. Close all windows.

End of lab.

LAB 14
CONFIGURING AUTHORIZATION AND AUTHENTICATION

THIS LAB CONTAINS THE FOLLOWING EXERCISES AND ACTIVITIES:

Exercise 14.1 Creating and Managing a Local User Account

Exercise 14.2 Configuring a PIN and Picture Password

Exercise 14.3 Creating and Managing Domain User Accounts

Exercise 14.4 Using Credential Manager

Exercise 14.5 Configuring Device Guard and Credential Guard

Lab Challenge Managing Account Policies

BEFORE YOU BEGIN

The lab environment consists of student workstations connected to a local area network, along with a server that functions as the domain controller for a domain called adatum.com. The computers required for this lab are listed in Table 14-1.

Table 14-1
Computers required for Lab 14

Computer	Operating System	Computer Name
Server (VM 1)	Windows Server 2012 R2	LON-DC1
Client (VM 2)	Windows 10	LON-CL1

In addition to the computers, you will also require the software listed in Table 14-2 to complete Lab 14.

Table 14-2
Software required for Lab 14

Software	Location
Lab 14 student worksheet	Lab14_worksheet.docx (provided by instructor)

Working with Lab Worksheets

Each lab in this manual requires that you answer questions, shoot screen shots, and perform other activities that you will document in a worksheet named for the lab, such as Lab14_worksheet.docx. You will find these worksheets on the book companion site. It is recommended that you use a USB flash drive to store your worksheets, so you can submit them to your instructor for review. As you perform the exercises in each lab, open the appropriate worksheet file, fill in the required information, and then save the file to your flash drive.

SCENARIO

After completing this lab, you will be able to:

- Create and manage a local user account

- Configure passwords and PINs

- Create and manage domain user accounts

- Use Credential Manager

- Configure Device Guard and Credential Guard

- Manage account policies

Estimated lab time: 110 minutes

Exercise 14.1	Creating a Local User Account
Overview	In this exercise, you will create a new local user account. You will then manage the new user's password by using Settings and the Computer Management console.
Mindset	Authentication represents the way that security principals (users, computers, and processes) prove their identities before they are allowed to connect to your network. The most common authentication method is a password.
Completion time	25 minutes

1. Log on to **LON-CL1** as **adatum\administrator** with the password of **Pa$$w0rd**.

2. Right-click the **Start** button and choose **Computer Management**.

3. In the Computer Management console, expand the **Local Users and Groups** node and then click the **Users** node, as shown in Figure 14-1.

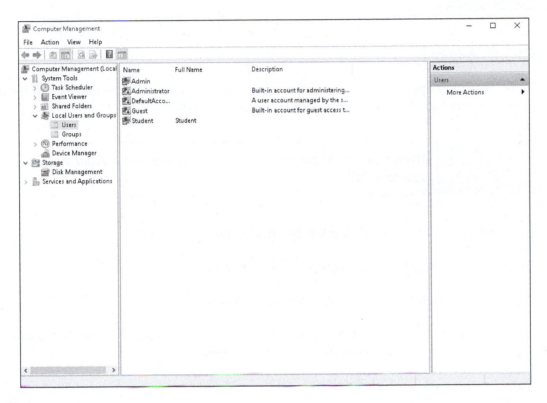

Figure 14-1
Managing local user accounts

4. Right-click the **Users** node and choose **New User**.

5. In the New User dialog box, type the following information and then click the **Create** button.

    User name: **JSmith**

    Full Name: **John Smith**

    Password and Confirm password: **Pa$$w0rd**

6. Click to deselect the **User must change password at next logon** option.

7. Click the **Close** button to close the New User dialog box.

8. Take a screen shot showing the Computer Management console showing the new user by pressing **Alt+PrtScr** and then paste it into your Lab14_worksheet file in the page provided by pressing **Ctrl+V**.

9. Double-click the **JSmith** account.

10. In the JSmith Properties dialog box, click the **Member Of** tab.

Question 1	Which group is JSmith a member of?

11. Click the **Add** button.

12. In the Select Groups dialog box, answer the following question, and then in the Enter the object names to select text box, type **Administrators** and click **OK**.

Question 2	Which location will the group come from based on the From this location field?

13. Close the JSmith Properties dialog box by clicking **OK**.

14. Right-click the JSmith account and choose **Set Password**.

15. In the Set Password for JSmith dialog box, click **Proceed**.

16. In the Set Password for JSmith dialog box, in the New password text box and the Confirm password text box, type **Password01** and then click **OK**.

17. Once the password is set, click **OK**.

18. Close the Computer Management console.

19. Click the **Start** button and then click **Settings**.

20. In the Settings window, click **Accounts**.

21. Click **Other users**. You should see the John Smith account.

22. Log out of Windows 10 by clicking the **Start** button, right-clicking **Administrator**, and then clicking **Sign out**.

23. At the bottom of the screen, click **Other user**. Then log on as **Lon-CL1\JSmith** with the password of **Password01**. It will take a couple minutes to create a profile for JSmith.

24. Click the **Start** button. Right-click **John Smith** and choose **Change account settings**.

25. Click **Sign-in options**.

26. In the Password section, click the **Change** button.

27. When you are prompted for the Current password, type **Password01** and then click **Next**.

28. In the New password text box and the Reenter password text box, type **Pa$$w0rd**. In the Password hint text box, type **Default**. Click **Next**.

29. Take a screen shot showing that the password was changed by pressing **Alt+PrtScr** and then paste it into your Lab14_worksheet file in the page provided by pressing **Ctrl+V**.

30. Click the **Finish** button.

Question 3	Which message appears?

Question 4	Since the password includes all four types of characters (making it a complex password) and is 8 characters long, what is the real reason this message appears?

31. Click **Close**.

32. Right-click the **Start** button and choose **Computer Management**.

33. In the Computer Management console, expand the **Local Users and Groups** node and then click the **Users** node.

34. Right-click the **JSmith** and account and choose **Set Password**.

35. In the Set Password for JSmith dialog box, click the **Proceed** button.

36. In the New password text box and the Confirm password text box, type **Pa$$w0rd** and then click **OK**.

37. Once the password has been set, click **OK**.

38. Close **Computer Management**.

Leave LON-CL1\JSmith open for the next exercise but close the Settings window.

Exercise 14.2	Configuring a PIN and Picture Password
Overview	In this exercise, you will configure a PIN and picture password for the new account you just created in Exercise 14.1.
Mindset	Two other forms of authentication based on what you know is the personal identification number (PIN) and picture password. A PIN is a short numeric password used to authenticate a user to a system. A picture password consists of two components: a picture and a gesture that you draw on it. You can pick the image from a default set included with the Windows 10 installation or you can select your own.
Completion time	20 minutes

1. While logged on to LON-CL1 as JSmith, click the **Start** button and then click **Settings**.

2. Click **Accounts**.

3. Click **Sign-in options**, as shown in Figure 14-2.

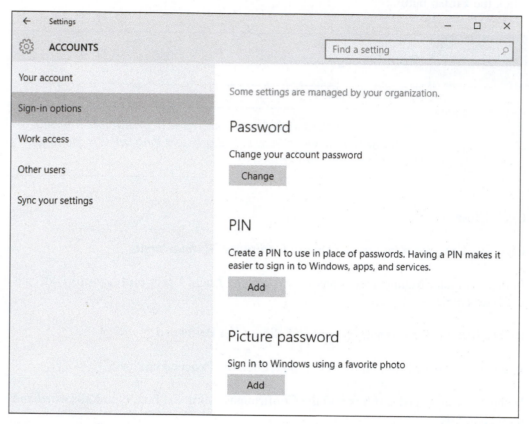

Figure 14-2
Managing local user accounts

4. In the PIN section, click the **Add** button.

5. On the First, verify your account password page, in the text box, type **Pa$$w0rd** and then click **OK**.

6. On the Set up a PIN page, in the New PIN text box and Confirm PIN text box, type **1234** and then click **OK**.

7. Take a screen shot showing the Accounts page by pressing **Alt+PrtScr** and then paste it into your Lab14_worksheet file in the page provided by pressing **Ctrl+V**.

8. Log out of Windows 10.

9. Log on again as John Smith, but instead of providing a password, click **Sign-in Options**.

Question 5	*What are the two options can you use to login with?*

10. In the PIN text box, type **1234**.

Question 6	*Which is more secure, passwords or PINs? Explain your answer.*

11. Click the **Start** button and then click **Settings**.

12. Click **Accounts**.

13. Click **Sign-in options**.

14. To delete a PIN, in the PIN section, click **Remove**.

15. When you are prompted to confirm that you want to remove your PIN, click the **Remove** button. You may need to scroll down to see the Remove button.

16. On the First, verify your account password page, in the Password text box, type **Pa$$w0rd** and then click **OK**.

17. In the Picture password section, click the **Add** button.

18. On the Create a picture password page, in the text box, type **Pa$$Word** and then click **OK**.

19. On the Welcome to picture password page, click **Choose Picture**.

20. In the Open dialog box, navigate to **C:\ProgramData\Microsoft\Windows NT\MSScan** and then click the **WelcomeScan** picture. Click **Open**. If you don't see the C:\ProgramData folder, in the File name text box, type **C:\ProgramData** and then press **Enter** to get you started. The ProgramData is a hidden folder.

21. Click **Use this Picture**.

22. Draw three gestures on your picture, as shown on Figure 14-3. Be patient when drawing the gesture three times. Just make sure the start and end points are the same each time.

Figure 14-3
Defining gestures

23. On the Congratulations page, take a screen shot by pressing **Alt+PrtScr** and then paste it into your Lab14_worksheet file in the page provided by pressing **Ctrl+V**.

24. Click **Finish**.

25. Log out of Windows 10.

26. Log on with the user account using the picture password.

27. Click the **Start** button, click **Settings**, and then click **Accounts**.

28. On the Accounts page, click **Sign-in options**.

29. In the Picture password section, click the **Remove** button.

30. Close the Settings window.

Remain logged in for the next exercise.

Exercise 14.3	Creating and Managing Domain User Accounts
Overview	In this exercise, you will use Active Directory Users and Computers to create a domain account. You will then provide domain account access to a computer running Windows 10.
Mindset	A domain is a collection of user and computer accounts that are grouped together to enable centralized management and to apply security. The user and computer accounts are stored in an Active Directory database that is stored on domain controllers. The domain-based accounts provide access to resources on multiple systems.
Completion time	25 minutes

1. Log on to **LON-DC1** as **adatum\administrator** with the password of **Pa$$w0rd**.

2. On **LON-DC1**, in Server Manager, click **Tools > Active Directory Users and Computers**.

3. In the Active Directory Users and Computers console, expand the **Adatum.com** node and then click the **Users** node (see Figure 14-4).

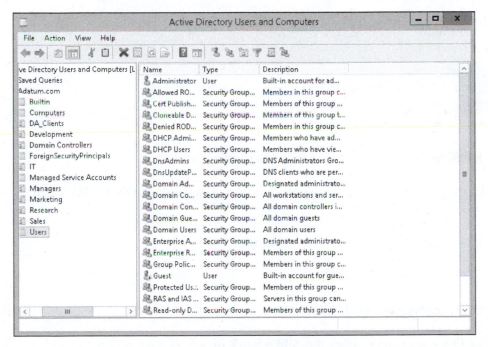

Figure 14-4
Managing users with Active Directory Users and Computers

4. Right-click the **Users** node and choose **New > User**.

5. In the New Object – User dialog box, type the following information and then click **Next**:

First name: **Tay**

Last name: **Inham**

Full name: **Tay Inham**

User logon name: **TInham**

User logon name: **TInham**

6. In the Password text box and the Confirm password text box, type **Pa$$w0rd.**

7. Click to deselect the **User must change password at next logon** option and then click **Next**.

8. Take a screen shot showing the new object to be created by pressing **Alt+PrtScr** and then paste it into your Lab14_worksheet file in the page provided by pressing **Ctrl+V**.

9. Click **Finish**.

10. Right-click the new user that you just created and choose **Properties**.

11. In the Tay Inham Properties dialog box, click the **Member Of** tab.

Question 7	Which group is the new user a member of?

12. Click **OK** to close the Tay Inham Properties dialog box.

13. On **LON-CL1**, if you are not logged on as JSmith, log on as **LON-CL1\JSmith** with the password of **Pa$$w0rd**.

14. Click the **Start** buton and then click **Settings**.

15. In the Settings window, click **Accounts**.

16. On the Accounts page, click **Other users**.

17. On the Other users page, click the **Add a work or school user** option.

18. When the Account info is open, in the User account text box, type **adatum\TInham**. For the Account type, select **Administrator** and then click **Add**.

19. Take a screen shot showing the Other users page by pressing **Alt+PrtScr** and then paste it into your Lab14_worksheet file in the page provided by pressing **Ctrl+V**.

20. Close the Settings window.

21. Log off LON-CL1.

22. On **LON-CL1,** when the logon screen appears, click **Other user**. Then log on as **adatum\ TInham** with the password of **Pa$$w0rd**.

23. When you are prompted to change the password, click **OK**.

24. In the New password text box and the Confirm passwword text box, type **Password01** and press **Enter**.

25. When the password has been changed, click **OK**.

26. Click **Sign in**.

27. Right-click the **Start** button and choose **Computer Management**.

28. Expand the **Local Users and Groups** node and then click **Groups**.

29. Double-click the **Adminsitrators** group.

Question 8	Which groups and users are part of the Administrators group?

30. Close the Administrators Properties dialog box by clicking **OK**.

Leave LON-CL1 open for the next exercise.

Exercise 14.4	Using Credential Manager
Overview	In this exercise, you will use Credential Manager to manage the credentials for users when they accesss servers and websites.
Mindset	Credential Manager allows you to store credentials (such as user names and passwords) that you use to log on to websites or other computers on a network. By storing your credentials, Windows can automatically log you on to websites or other computers. Credentials are saved in special folders on your computer called vaults.
Completion time	10 minutes

1. On LON-CL1, right-click the **Start** button and choose **Control Panel**.

2. In the Control Panel, click **User Accounts > Credential Manager**. The Credential Manager control panel applet appears, as shown in Figure 14-5.

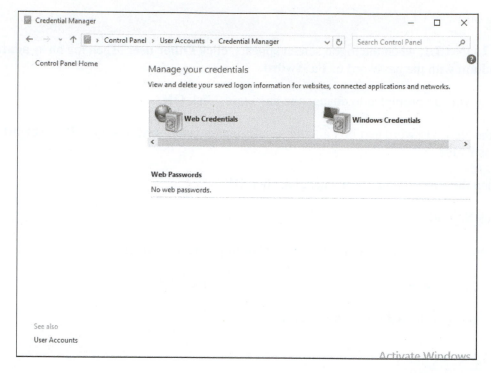

Figure 14-5
Managing stored credentials

3. Click **Windows Credentials** and then click **Add a Windows credential**. The Add a Windows Credential dialog box appears.

4. In the Internet or network address text box, type **\\RemotePC**.

5. In the User name text box, type **Administrator**.

6. In the Password text box, type **Pa$$w0rd** and then click **OK**. The credential appears in the Windows Credentials list. Now any time that you access the \\RemotePC, you will use the username administrator with the password of Pa$$w0rd.

7. Take a screen shot of the Windows Credentials control panel showing the new credential you entered by pressing **Ctrl+PrtScr** and then paste the resulting image into the Lab14_worksheet file in the page provided by pressing **Ctrl+V**.

Question 9	Describe how to move your saved credentials from one computer to another.

Exercise 14.5	Configuring Device Guard and Credential Guard
Overview	In this exercise, you will enable Device Guard and Credential Guard, which help protect the system against malware.
Mindset	Device Guard is a group of key features that hardens a computer system against malware by only running trusted applications, thereby preventing malicious code from running. Credential Guard isolates and hardens key system and user security information. However, both technologies are available only with Windows 10 Enterprise.
Completion time	15 minutes

1. On LON-CL1, log off Windows. Then log back on to LON-CL1 as **adatum\administrator** with the password of **Pa$$w0rd**.

2. On LON-CL1, verify that client Hyper-V is installed. If it is not, perform the following steps:

   a. On LON-CL1, right-click the **Start** button and choose **Command Prompt (Admin)**.

   b. Execute the following two commands.

   ```
   Dism /online /enable-feature /featurename:
   Microsoft-Hyper-V /All
   ```

   c. When you are prompted to reboot, press the **y** key.

   d. Log back on to LON-CL1 as **adatum\administrator** with the password of **Pa$$w0rd**.

3. Right-click the **Start** button and choose **Programs and Features**.

4. Click the **Turn Windows features on or off** option.

5. In the Windows Features dialog box, select **Isolated User Mode** and then click **OK**.

6. When you are prompted to to restart the computer, click the **Restart now** option.

7. Log back on to LON-CL1 as **adatum\administrator** with the password of **Pa$$w0rd**.

8. Click the **Start** button, type **gpedit.msc**, and then press **Enter,** In the Group Policy Management Editor, expand the screen (see Figure 14-6).

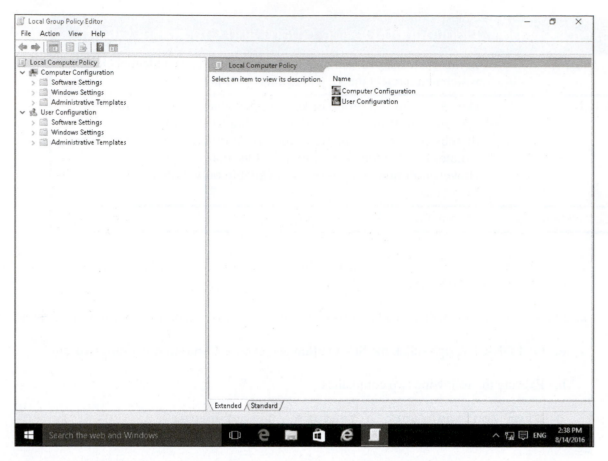

Figure 14-6
Opening the Local Group Policy Editor

9. Navigate to the **Computer Configuration\Administrative Templates\System\Device Guard** node. Then double-click **Turn On Virtualization Based Security**.

10. In the Turn on Virtualization Based Security dialog box, select the **Enabled** option.

Question 10	What is the Security Platform Security Level set to?

11. To enable Device Guard, select the **Enable Virtualization Based Protection of Code Integrity** option.

12. To enable Credential Guard, select the **Enable with UEFI lock** option.

13. Take a screen shot of the Turn on Virtualization Based Security settings by pressing **Ctrl+PrtScr** and then paste the resulting image into the Lab14_worksheet file in the page provided by pressing **Ctrl+V**.

14. Close the Turn on Virtualization Based Security dialog box by clicking **OK**.

Lab Challenge	Managing Account Policies
Overview	In this exercise, you will define a domain-level password policy, including configuring maximum password length and password history.
Mindset	You can define only account policies—which include password policy, account lockout policy, and Kerberos policy—at the domain level. Because most organizations have only one domain, you can set only one.
Completion time	15 minutes

1. Log on to **LON-DC1** as **adatum\administrator** with the password of **Pa$$w0rd**.

2. On **LON-DC1**, in **Server Manager**, click **Tools > Group Policy Management**. The Group Policy Management console opens.

3. Expand the **Forest: Adatum.com** node, expand the **Domains** node, and then click the **Adatum.com** node.

4. Right-click **Default Domain Policy** and choose **Edit**. The Group Policy Management Editor opens.

5. In the left window pane, expand the **Computer Configuration** node, expand the **Policies** node, and then expand the **Windows Settings** folder. Then expand the **Security Settings** node. In the Security Settings node, expand **Account Policies** and click **Password Policy**, as shown in Figure 14-7.

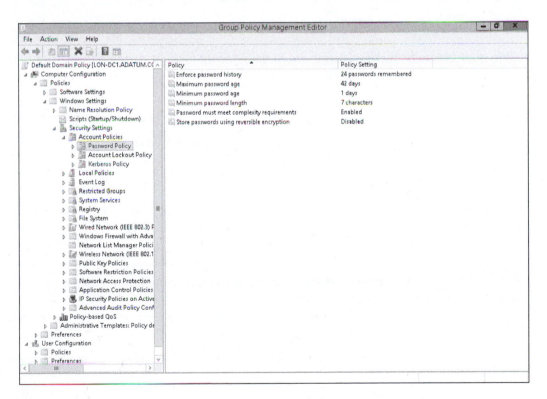

Figure 14-7
Managing GPOs

Question 11	What is the maximum password age?

Question 12	What is the minimum password length?

Question 13	How does enforce password history and minimum password age work together to keep a network environment secure?

6. Double-click **Minimum password length**. In the Minimum password length Properties dialog box, change the 7 value to **8** characters. Click **OK** to close the Minimum password length Properties dialog box.

7. Take a screen shot of the Group Policy Management Editor window by pressing **Alt+PrtScr** and then paste it into your Lab14_worksheet file in the page provided by pressing **Ctrl+V**.

8. Under Account Policies, click **Account Lockout Policy**.

Question 14	How are the account lockout settings currently set?

9. Double-click **Account lockout duration**. In the Account lockout duration Properties dialog box, click to enable the **Define this policy setting**.

Question 15	What is the default value for the Account lockout duration?

10. Click **OK** to close the Account lockout duration Properties dialog box. In the Suggested Value Changes dialog box, look at the suggested settings and then click **OK**.

Question 16	How many invalid logon attempts can be made that will cause an account to be locked?

11. Take a screen shot of the Account Lockout Policy window by pressing **Alt+PrtScr** and then paste it into your Lab14_worksheet file in the page provided by pressing **Ctrl+V**.

12. Close the Group Policy Management Editor window for the Default Domain Policy and then close the Group Policy Management console.

End of lab.

LAB 15
CONFIGURING ADVANCED MANAGEMENT TOOLS

THIS LAB CONTAINS THE FOLLOWING EXERCISES AND ACTIVITIES:

Exercise 15.1   Configuring Services

Exercise 15.2   Using System Configuration Management Utility

Exercise 15.3   Using Task Scheduler

Lab Challenge   Creating a Windows PowerShell Script

BEFORE YOU BEGIN

The lab environment consists of student workstations connected to a local area network, along with a server that functions as the domain controller for a domain called adatum.com. The computers required for this lab are listed in Table 15-1.

Table 15-1
Computers required for Lab 15

Computer	Operating System	Computer Name
Server (VM 1)	Windows Server 2012 R2	LON-DC1
Client (VM 3)	Windows 10	LON-CL1

In addition to the computers, you will also require the software listed in Table 15-2 to complete Lab 15.

Table 15-2

Software required for Lab 15

Software	Location
Lab 15 student worksheet	Lab15_worksheet.docx (provided by instructor)

Working with Lab Worksheets

Each lab in this manual requires that you answer questions, shoot screen shots, and perform other activities that you will document in a worksheet named for the lab, such as Lab15_worksheet.docx. You will find these worksheets on the book companion site. It is recommended that you use a USB flash drive to store your worksheets, so you can submit them to your instructor for review. As you perform the exercises in each lab, open the appropriate worksheet file, fill in the required information, and then save the file to your flash drive.

SCENARIO

After completing this lab, you will be able to:

- Configure services

- Use System Configuration Management Utility

- Use Task Scheduling

- Create a Windows PowerShell Script with Windows PowerShell ISE

Estimated lab time: 70 minutes

Exercise 15.1	Configuring Services
Overview	In this exercise, you will create a service account that will be used to run a service. You will then manage a service, including restarting the service.
Mindset	Services are programs that run in the background on a Windows system to provide a function or a network application or to help the operating system run other programs. Services are managed using the Services console, which can be opened by executing services.msc.
Completion time	30 minutes

1. Log on to **LON-CL1** as **adatum\administrator** with the password of **Pa$$w0rd**.

2. Right-click the Start button and choose **Computer Management**.

3. In the Computer Management console, expand the **Local Users and Groups** node and then click **Users**.

4. Right-click the **Users** tab and choose **New User**.

5. In the New User dialog box, type the following information:

   User name: **Service-Account**

   Password and Confirm password: **Pa$$w0rd**

6. Click to deselect the **User must change password at next logon** option and then select the **Password never expires** option.

7. Click the **Create** button and then click the **Close** button.

8. Double-click **Service-Account**.

9. In the Service-Account Properties dialog box, click the **Member Of** tab.

10. Click the **Add** button.

11. In the Select Groups dialog box, in the Enter the object names to select text box, type **administrators** and then click **OK**.

12. Close the Service-Account Properties dialog box by clicking the **OK** button.

13. Click **Start** and then type **services.msc**. From the results, click **Services**.

14. In the Services console, in the details pane, double-click the **Print Spooler**. The service's Properties dialog box displays, as shown in Figure 15-1.

Figure 15-1
Managing Print Spooler services

15. On the General tab, click the **Startup type** drop-down list.

Question 1	What are the four startup options?

16. For the Startup type, select **Manual**.

17. Click the **Log On** tab.

Question 2	What is the log on account?

18. Select the **This account** option.

19. Click the **Browse** button. In the Select User dialog box, in the Enter the object name to select text box, type **Service-Account**.

20. Take a screen shot of the Log On tab by pressing **Alt+PrtScr** and then paste it into your Lab15_worksheet file in the page provided by pressing **Ctrl+V**.

21. Close the Print Spooler Properties dialog box by clicking **OK**.

22. In the Password text box and the Confirm password text boxe, type **Pa$$w0rd** and then click OK.

23. When the Service-Account has been granted the Log On As a Service right, click **OK**.

24. When a message indicates that the new logon name will not take effect util you stop and restart the service, click **OK**.

25. Reboot **LON-CL1**.

26. Log on to **LON-CL1** as **adatum\administrator** with the password of **Pa$$w0rd**.

27. Click **Start** and type **services.msc**. From the results, click **Services**.

28. Double-click the **Print Spooler** service.

Question 3	What is the status of the service?

29. Click the **Start** button.

Question 4	Which error message appears?

30. Close the Services dialog box by clicking **OK**.

31. Back on the General tab, change the Startup type to **Automatic**.

32. Click the **Log On** tab.

33. Select the **Local System account** and then click **OK**.

34. Right-click the **Print Spooler** service and choose **Start**.

    Close the Services console. Leave LON-CL1 open for the next exercise.

Exercise 15.2	Using System Configuration Management Utility
Overview	In this exercise, you will configure startup options using the System Configuration Management Utility.
Mindset	The System Configuration Management Utility (msconfig.exe) lets you enable or disable startup services, set boot options (such as booting into Safe Mode), access tools like Action Center and Event Viewer, and more. You'll use this utility mainly to troubleshoot startup problems with Windows.
Completion time	15 minutes

1. On **LON-CL1**, click the **Start** button, type **msconfig**, and then press **Enter**. The System Configuration utility opens (see Figure 15-2).

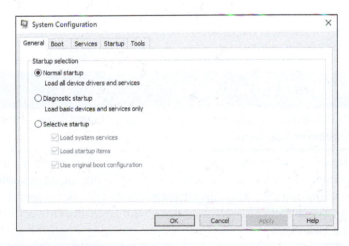

Figure 15-2
Opening the System Configuration utility

2. Click the **Boot** tab.

Question 5	What is the default operating system entry?

3. Select the **Safe boot** option.

4. Click the **Advanced options** button.

5. In the BOOT Advanced Options dialog box, select the Number of processors. Then for the number of processors, select **2**.

6. Select the **Maximum memory** option.

7. Close the BOOT Advanced Options dialog box by clicking **OK**.

8. Close System Configuration by clicking **OK**.

9. When you are prompted to restart the computer, click the **Restart** button.

10. Log on to **LON-CL1** as **adatum\administrator** with the password of **Pa$$w0rd**. If a message indicates that this app can't open, click **Close**.

11. Take a screen shot of system running in Safe mode by pressing **Alt+PrtScr** and then paste it into your Lab15_worksheet file in the page provided by pressing **Ctrl+V**.

12. Right-click the **Start** button and click **Command Prompt (Admin)**.

13. In the Administrator: Command Prompt window, type **msconfig** and then press **Enter**.

14. In the System Configuration dialog box select the **Normal startup** option and then click **OK**.

15. When you are prompted to restart the computer, click the **Restart** button.

Leave LON-CL1 open for the next exercise.

Exercise 15.3	Using Task Scheduler
Overview	In this exercise, you will schedule a task that will start notepad whenever you logon.
Mindset	Task Scheduler enables you to schedule and automate a variety of actions, such as starting programs, displaying messages, and even sending e-mails. You can create a scheduled task by specifying a trigger (an event that causes a task to run) and an action (the action taken when the task runs).
Completion time	15 minutes

1. Log on to **LON-CL1** as **adatum\administrator** with the password of **Pa$$w0rd**.

2. Click the **Start** button and then type **Task Scheduler**. From the results, click **Task Scheduler**. Task Scheduler opens (see Figure 15-3).

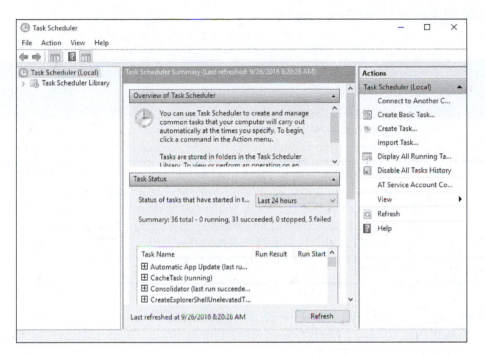

Figure 15-3
Task Scheduler

3. In the Actions pane on the right, click **Create Basic Task**.

4. In the Create Basic Task Wizard, in the Name text box, type **Notepad Startup** and then click **Next**.

5. On the Task Trigger page, select the **When I log on** option and then click **Next**.

6. On the Action page, the Start a program option is selected. Click **Next**.

7. On the Start a Program page, in the Program/script text box, type **notepad** and then click **Next**.

8. On the Summary screen, click **Finish**.

9. Log off LON-CL1 and log back on to LON-CL1 as **adatum\administrator** with the password of **Pa$$w0rd**.

10. Take a screen shot of Notepad by pressing **Alt+PrtScr** and then paste it into your Lab15_worksheet file in the page provided by pressing **Ctrl+V**.

11. Close **Notepad**.

12. Click **Start** and then type **Task Scheduler**. From the results, click **Task Scheduler**.

13. Click the **Task Scheduler Library** node.

14. Right-click the **Notepad Startup** task and choose **Delete**. When you are prompted to confirm that you are sure, click **Yes**.

Leave LON-CL1 open for the next exercise.

Lab Challenge	Creating a Windows PowerShell Script
Overview	In this exercise, you will create a simple script that will display the operating systme version, build number, and serial number.
Mindset	PowerShell is a powerful tool used to manage and configure Windows. Windows 10 includes the Windows PowerShell Integrated Scripting Environment (ISE) that helps you create Windows PowerShell scripts. If you need the scripts to be executed on a regular basis, you can execute the scripts using Task Scheduler.
Completion time	10 minutes

1. On **LON-CL1**, click **Start** and then type **powershell ISE**. Then from the results, click **PowerShell ISE**. Click the **Script** down arrow button, to show Untitled1.ps1, as shown in Figure 15-4.

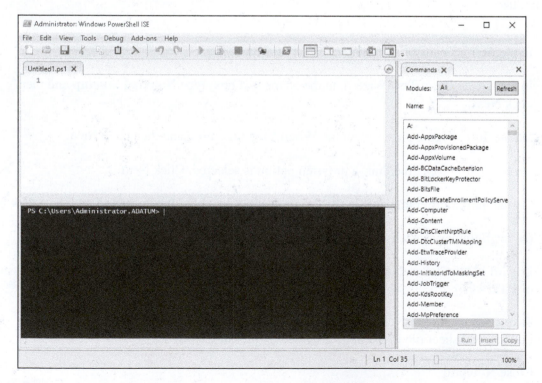

Figure 15-4
Opening Windows PowerShell ISE

Question 6	*What is the default script?*

2. In the Untitled1.ps1 tab box, type the following lines:

   ```
   Get-WmiObject -Class win32_OperatingSystem

   -ComputerName localhost

   Select-Object -Property CSName,LastBootUpTime
   ```

3. On the Windows PowerShell ISE toolbar, click the **Save** button.

4. In the File name text box, type **Script1.ps1** and click the **Save** button.

5. On the Windows PowerShell ISE toolbar, click the **Run Script** button (green arrow).

6. Take a screen shot of the Windows PowerShell ISE window by pressing **Alt+PrtScr** and then paste it into your Lab15_worksheet file in the page provided by pressing **Ctrl+V**.

7. Log off LON-CL1

End of lab.